There is no
such thing as
Death

2

There is no
such thing as
Death

Evidence for eternal life
that you can verify
for yourself

A. Zimmerman, PhD

To request permissions, contact the author
azimmermanphd@gmail.com

ISBN: 979-8398819625

First paperback edition June 2017
published under the pen name R.C. Clarence

Kindle Direct Publishing

Dedication

This book is dedicated to all my teachers, with special thanks to C.W. Leadbeater, whose life-long work in the field of clairvoyant investigation pioneered a new era of peace and hope for all humanity.

How to read the 2nd edition

This is the kind of book in which the material builds upon itself from chapter to chapter. For that reason, it is suggested to **start with the Introduction, then proceed to Chapters 1, 2, 3, etc.**

To help with comprehension, key points are italicized and bolded or underlined throughout. Since these ideas will be new to most people, *it is recommended readers familiarize themselves with the chart titled "The 7 Planes of Consciousness" in chapter 1 and bookmark it or take a picture with your phone for easy reference.* This procedure is suggested because discussions about the after-death states will be based on an understanding of that chart.

As for the material presented in the chapters, it should be viewed as an introductory text designed to give the reader a solid foundation upon which they may build. If greater detail is desired, there is a suggested reading list that appears at the end.

Further, I am not asking anyone to believe the concepts presented in this book simply because I know many of them to be true based on personal experience. But I do request readers consider them as working hypotheses that have some common sense behind them. From there, you can proceed to verify the facts for yourself; and the methods describing how to verify the teachings are included in the final chapter.

In all matters like this, students approaching the higher truths of life are taught to avoid contempt before investigation. In other words, give it a fair chance. Then, accept or reject it as you see fit.

This second edition of the book contains minor corrections and edits. The format and content remain essentially the same as the first edition which I published in 2017 under the pen name R. C. Clarence.

Table of Contents

A scientific approach to the afterlife. Trained
clairvoyance. Clairvoyance as birthright of humanity.
The Great White Lodge. The Theosophical Society.

The Basics

The 7 planes of consciousness. Creation of the
universe. Evolution of a solar system. The Absolute.
The Supreme Being. The Solar Deity. We are not alone
in the universe. Creation of the human spirit. Life
forces and energy vampires. Origin of thoughts and
emotions. The Law of Evolution. The Law of Rebirth.
The Law of Karma.

The Meaning of Life and Death

Life as a school of experience. The secret to a happy life.
Sleep and astral travel. Talking with the "dead" at night.

Death as transfer of consciousness. The material body.
The etheric double. The astral body. The mental body.
The second and third "deaths". Life spans of our
various bodies.

What Really Happens on the Other Side

Learning karmic lessons. The need for silence after death.
Ghosts and the soul in the "grey world".
The etheric corpse.

Higher vibrational existence. Expansion of consciousness.
Speed of astral travel. 4 dimensional space.
7 sub-planes. The underworld. Ghosts and "lost souls".
The "Summer Land" or first Heaven. End of astral life.

Home of the second and third Heavens. The 7 sub-planes.
Life in the traditional Heaven (second Heaven). The third
Heaven, home of the soul. Reincarnation. Soul ages.
Planning our next life. Our immortality.

How to Verify the Wisdom Tradition for Yourself

Improving powers of observation. Definition of
clairvoyance. True yoga practice. The "lower self" and
the "Higher Self". Purification. Attracting a teacher.
Meditation. What to expect. Time to development of
clairvoyance. The yoga culture – choose carefully.
Dangers of kundalini yoga. Opening the door to a new
life.

Acknowledgements

This book would not have been possible without the tireless work of early members of the Theosophical Society, including Madame Blavatsky, Col. Henry Steel Olcott, Dr. Annie Besant, and Bishop Charles W. Leadbeater.

As a team, Dr. Annie Besant and Bishop C.W. Leadbeater made most of the clairvoyant investigations into the nature of the afterlife that are reported in this book. In fact, during the 40 years of their research into people that crossed over, they were able to examine several thousand individuals.[1] It has simply been my privilege and calling in this life to synthesize the great work they did into a modern, easy-to-read summary of the basic principles underlying the structure of our solar system and the nature of life and death.

∞ Introduction ∞

The Wisdom Tradition

A scientific approach to the afterlife

What you are about to read will probably be surprising. You are going to find definite facts taking the place of the mass of speculation and uncertainty surrounding death. The widespread confusion about the afterlife is natural considering that our cultural programming tells us death is some dark unknown, and no one *really* knows what happens when we die. In fact, ***the idea that death is a fear-filled unknown is one of the most persistent and destructive lies that have been perpetuated in the West for over a thousand years.*** And this fear-filled idea of death has caused tremendous suffering – both in this world and on the other side.

To start, I ask you to suspend any pre-judgments you may have about the afterlife until you review the concepts presented. The findings described in this book are not a story based on the author's personal experience; nor is it a story based on the reports of people who have had near-death experiences. Instead, ***the material presented in this book is based on our widely accepted scientific method,*** which involves repeated observations –

painstakingly made, noted and tabulated – by people carefully trained in their field of study. In this case, the field of study is the after-death states, and the facts compiled are based on thousands of observations of individuals on the other side. (1) (2)

Trained clairvoyance

The simplest explanation for the origin of the facts presented in this book is that they were observed and catalogued through the use of clairvoyant abilities. And by clairvoyant abilities, I am not referring to the degraded concepts of clairvoyance that have come to be associated with fortune telling, ghost stories, or predictions of wealth and romance for a fee; but rather *trained clairvoyance, which involves the slow and steady development of abilities that lie dormant within every one of us under the guidance of a qualified teacher* – a process that requires at least a year of intensive, uninterrupted practice. (3)

There are many individuals who have some degree of psychic ability, but trained clairvoyants are extremely rare. As a rule, trained clairvoyants are the most humble people in the world. In addition, they have sworn to use their abilities for the betterment of humanity and never for selfish ends. Therefore, you won't find them advertising the use of their abilities for a fee.

The information presented in this book has been gathered using the method of trained clairvoyance just mentioned. And while this might sound incredible to those who are unfamiliar with the wealth of information that can be obtained with psychic abilities, if you keep an open mind, my hope is that you will understand the process better by the end of the book. *The number one thing to realize is that clairvoyance is not some rare gift possessed by a few individuals, but simply the extension of our ability to perceive the world around us.*

This extension of current powers of observation allows us to become sensitive to a wider range of vibrations from the world. And, as strange as it may sound to the average person, *there are higher-vibrational, extra-dimensional realms of existence all around us – right here and right now – but we simply haven't awakened the ability to perceive them.* However, as we develop clairvoyance, we start to become conscious of these higher realms. And from the study of what we see, it is possible to learn a great deal more about the nature of existence, including what we commonly call life and death.

The only reason more people don't work on developing these gifts is because most of us in the West have been told that these abilities are "not normal ". Or that we need to be born into a family with psychic abilities. But everyone can think of some friend or family member who has had at least a touch of "higher sight". Examples range from the single occurrence of seeing, hearing or feeling the presence of a loved one who recently crossed over – often called a "ghost" – through regular glimpses of non-physical events.

This state of affairs is natural, since we are at a stage in human evolution in which it takes a good deal of discipline and training to awaken clairvoyance; though the road is open to anyone who is willing to make the effort. But today, more than ever, there are people born into the world who are highly intuitive and sensitive. And if you are one of those people, it will be even easier for you to awaken clairvoyant abilities. But no matter what level of clairvoyance you possess, the material in this book is designed to give you practical and definite guidance on your path toward psychic development.

As for the methods of developing clairvoyant abilities, we'll cover those details in chapter 7. For now, suffice it to say that these powers are real, and that they are being used by a growing number of people on the planet on a daily basis. And, *for the simple fact that the majority of people who have an experience of the afterlife are untrained observers of the higher realms of existence, we can account for the different versions of what they report.* For example, thought is creative on the other side, so what we think about, takes form. Therefore, people who hold certain religious beliefs often see glimpses of scenes or religious figures that are consistent with their expectations.

For those few clairvoyants that have undergone training, there is no haphazard or chaotic structure on the other side. And what they've found is there is a definite system of progression from lower to higher levels of consciousness after we cross over. These levels have sometimes been called planes, or worlds, or realms. (*In this book we will use the term planes for simplicity*). The term doesn't matter, pick whatever works for you. What does matter is there is a steady progression from the lower physical plane up to higher planes of existence after death in which we assimilate all that we have learned from the life just ended. Then, once this assimilation process is finished, we spend a significant amount of time planning for our next descent into physical life in order to gain new experience. *And this process of rebirth repeats itself over eons of time, and on multiple levels of existence, as part of an infinite process of experiencing, sharing and becoming.* (We'll take a detailed look at this as we move through the book)

Perception of the higher planes is just an extension of our current experience

It is a scientific fact – and we all know from daily experience – that we only perceive a small portion of the vibrations that come to us from the world we live in. For example, a certain range of vibrations perceived with our ears we call *sound*. And another set of much faster vibrations perceived by our eyes we call *visible light*.

So, it should be no great leap of faith to realize that even here on the physical plane there are many vibrations – both lower and higher than sound or light – that go unnoticed simply because our senses can't perceive them (like radio, TV and cell phone signals). We can easily confirm this by looking at any chart of the electromagnetic spectrum that shows just how small a portion of the frequencies are listed as "visible light". In fact, the vast majority of vibrations we are surrounded by on the physical plane go unnoticed simply because we can't see or hear them. And based on these facts, we are now able to understand the teaching that states, **the development of clairvoyance is simply becoming sensitive to a greater range of vibrations than the average person**.

Clairvoyance is your birthright

You might find it surprising to learn that every human being has the ability to expand his or her sensitivity to include a wider range of these vibrations until we begin to see more and more of these unseen worlds. This is your birthright, and this higher perception will eventually come to every one of us in the slow course of human evolution. But we all have the ability to develop these higher senses sooner through persistent hard work along specific lines that will be described in the last chapter of the book.

As for anyone who still doubts the existence of clairvoyant abilities, I can do no better than offer a quote from C.W. Leadbeater's book, **Man, Visible and Invisible**, *par. 8-10*

> *I am perfectly aware that the world at large is not yet convinced of the existence of this power of clairvoyant*

sight; but I also know that all who have really studied the question have found the evidence for it irresistible. If any intelligent person will read the authenticated stories quoted in my book Clairvoyance, and will then turn from them to the books from which they were selected, [he or she] will see at once that there is an overwhelming mass of evidence in favor of the existence of this faculty. To those who themselves can see, and are daily in the habit of exercising this higher vision in a hundred different ways, the denial of the majority that such sight is possible naturally seems ridiculous. For the clairvoyant the question is not worth arguing. If a blind man came up to us and assured us that there was no such thing as ordinary physical sight, and that we were deluded in supposing that we possessed this faculty, we in our turn should probably not feel it worthwhile to argue at great length in defense of our supposed delusion. We should simply say: "I certainly do see, and it is useless to try to persuade me that I do not; all the daily experiences of my life show me that I do; I decline to be argued out of my definite knowledge of positive facts." Now this is precisely how the trained clairvoyant feels when ignorant people serenely pronounce that it is quite impossible that he should possess a power which he is at that very moment using to read the thoughts of those who deny it to him.

For anyone who is still skeptical on the matter, or for those who are interested in more details on the material presented in this book, a suggested reading list appears at the end.

The existence of the Great White Lodge

We now come to a fact that still remains a mystery to most people – but which is key to our understanding of the concepts in this book – and that is the existence of the Great White Lodge. The Great White Lodge is simply a group of very highly developed individuals who stay in touch with earth to help inspire and guide humanity along its evolutionary path. *(And just to be clear, the word "white" has nothing to do with race. It only means that its members follow the "white path", which requires selfless work for the good of humanity, as opposed to those who follow the "dark path" and use clairvoyant powers for selfish ends).* The White Lodge has representatives from many countries around the world. And although it has sometimes been referred to as the Himalayan Lodge, because a few of its members live in Tibet, it would be incorrect to imagine some great monastery hidden away in the mountains. In fact, its members are scattered across the world so they can best serve the nations in which they live.

I am sure all this may sound astonishing to anyone who hasn't heard about the White Lodge before, but its existence follows from a very logical sequence of spiritual development. ***There have always been highly advanced men and women on earth who have developed their powers of strength, love and intelligence to such a high degree that they have stood far above average humanity.*** They were known as the high intellects, the saints, or the great altruistic leaders of humanity. Some of these people, through hard work and selfless service to others, achieved such a high level of spiritual consciousness that they met the evolutionary goal set for humanity far in advance of the general population. These people have sometimes been referred to as Ascended Masters or Masters of the Wisdom. But in the language of today, we could just imagine them as super high achievers.

Let's take a look at an analogy that might better explain what happens with these high achievers:

I'm sure each of us has heard stories about those rare, gifted children who become musical geniuses at age 12, or who go away to college at a young age and graduate with a PhD by age 18. Well, the process of early development that we are talking about is exactly the same, except that members of the White Lodge are individuals that have reached a high degree of spiritual achievement far in advance of the rest of humanity.

These great souls – who are no longer required to take birth again on earth – find there are seven paths open to them for their further advancement. Most of these paths take them far away from the earth to work in realms that we can only speculate upon. But one of the seven paths allows them to stay in touch with humanity and work for its benefit. This path is considered a very great sacrifice because, instead of moving fully into the bliss of the higher planes, these individuals have chosen to stay in touch with earth and all its suffering in order to help the rest of us. But their choice comes with great distinction and the true inner joy that results from helping others.

These advanced souls that choose to stay in touch with the earth to help humanity are the members that make up the Great White Lodge. They are always in the background, working to help us and protect the earth, but never interfering with humanity's free will. That is why we don't hear much about them. However, from time to time they do make efforts to put forward ideas that help reshape the world. For example, they inspired the founding of the Theosophical Society whose purpose was to introduce the Wisdom Tradition to the West.

This leads us to a couple of important points to take away from the existence of the White Lodge:

1. *Humanity is not struggling alone. There is always guidance and help waiting, if we sincerely ask for it.*
2. *From time to time the members of the White Lodge share their knowledge of the inner workings of life for the upliftment of humanity. In fact, much of the information included in this book regarding the structure of the universe and the planes of our solar system comes from some of their advanced pupils*

Keep in mind that **highly advanced men and women have always walked on earth in every age, even today**. The only difference is now we know they don't just die and disappear, but some of them make the great sacrifice of choosing to stay in touch with humanity in order to help. And that should be a very encouraging thought!

Inspiration for this book

Now that we know a little bit more about the method of trained clairvoyance that was used to gather the findings presented in this book, and about the existence of the Great White Lodge, let's get back to understanding more about the trained clairvoyants who initially investigated the after-death states. Most of the observations reported in this book were made from the mid 1890's through the 1930's by members of the Theosophical Society under the leadership of Dr. Annie Besant and Bishop Charles W. Leadbeater, two of the greatest clairvoyants of modern history.

The Theosophical Society was founded in New York City in 1875 at the request of two of the Masters of Wisdom in order to introduce the teachings of the Wisdom Tradition to the West. This tradition had long been taught in the East and was well known in ancient India. It was also known in the West as late as the classical periods in ancient Greece, Rome, and Egypt through the various mystery schools of the time. In them, students learned about the meaning of life and death, the origin of the solar system, and the great Spiritual Force behind it all. But during the dark ages, and continuing well into our modern era, the church banned all such teachings, so the keepers of this knowledge had to go underground. Today, we are fortunate enough to have the Wisdom Tradition taught publicly to anyone who is willing to take the time to learn its teachings and methods.

Theosophy and the Wisdom Tradition

The word Theosophy can be translated as "Divine Wisdom" from the Greek Theos=God, and Sophia=wisdom. For our purposes we will simply call it the Wisdom Tradition to avoid any misconceptions of it being some sort of religion, _which it most definitely is not_. The Wisdom Tradition belongs to the world. It requires no specific belief system. Anyone who studies it can keep his or her current beliefs – or non-beliefs. In fact, the Wisdom Tradition explains many of the confusing inconsistencies among the various religions and often gives them back to their believers on a much higher level, and with a much deeper understanding of the universal truths that underlie them all. What's more, **the Wisdom Tradition provides logical, scientific explanations for the structure of our universe and the purpose and meaning of life in a manner that is designed to appeal to people all across the spectrum, from religious people to agnostics to atheists.**

As an author, it is simply my privilege and calling in this life to take some of the basic teachings of the Wisdom Tradition and communicate them in today's language, and in a manner that makes sense to today's minds. Will it be perfect and complete in its presentation? No, simply because no account of all the possibilities of the afterlife ever can be. Even the original investigators cautioned that there is no claim to infallibility. But they did explain that every fact presented in their books was observed firsthand by at least two independent trained investigators and was further verified by more senior members who were much further advanced in their psychic abilities to check for accuracy. In addition, their findings were re-visited over a period of 40 years while their clairvoyant abilities were steadily growing; a period during which they had the opportunity to observe several thousand individuals on the other side. And even 40 years later, they found all the original facts presented were correct, and that only a few words had to be added.(4) What's more, the majority of the system that you are about to learn in this book was verified first-hand by one of these trained investigators.(5) And while no report of life on the other side can be perfect, the information presented in this book is highly reliable as far as it goes; and it definitely marks a significant advance over the popular accounts of the afterlife that are based on the experiences of untrained individual observers.

I hope you find this honesty reassuring because I have been taught that any presentation of great truths that asks us to believe blindly just because a certain religious figure said so – or because one great book or another said so – is asking us to give up our free will and our ability to know the truth for ourselves. Always we should decide for ourselves based on careful consideration of the facts presented, along with using our "internal teacher" – or intuition – which is active in the majority of people and speaks to us in moments of quiet contemplation.

What I propose to do in this book is tell you exactly why you can trust the facts presented. Not because I said so or because a team of trained investigators said so, but because you can verify them for yourself. In fact, you can become one of these qualified observers. That is one of the goals of this book; to set you on the path toward independence and discovery.

So let's get started. I hope you're as excited as I am to read on because the truth is magnificent and freeing beyond our wildest dreams. In fact, you'll find that the dead are all around us – right here and right now. They are much more alive than we are since they are free of the physical body; and they most definitely are not lying unconscious in the earth!

THE BASICS

∞ Chapter 1 ∞

The 7 Planes and the 3 Great Laws

The 7 planes of consciousness in our solar system

It is absolutely essential to our understanding of what happens after death to firmly grasp the idea that our solar system has 7 very distinct planes of consciousness; each plane consisting of many and varied opportunities for spiritual growth. The physical sun, the planets, and all the matter of the solar system as we know it exist on the lowest of the 7 planes, which is appropriately called the *Physical Plane.* There are 6 other planes of consciousness above and beyond the physical. So, gaining an understanding of the basic facts about the 7 planes of consciousness is going to be the key to our understanding of the afterlife, because each of us journeys through these higher planes after death.

To those of us who are completely focused on living in the physical world, the idea that there are other, higher states of consciousness may seem hard to believe. But our scientists know that something unseen is there – not just on earth, but throughout the whole universe – and they call it dark matter and dark energy (*not because it is "dark" in the sense of "lacking light", but because it is <u>unknown</u>*). What's more, NASA estimates this mysterious force-matter makes up about 95% of the known universe! (6)

But long before modern science acknowledged the existence of these vast unseen parts of the universe, highly advanced clairvoyants had observed some of the higher planes of nature that make up the other 95%. And when they did, they found out a great deal about the scheme of spiritual evolution in our own solar system and what happens to each of us after death.

The main things to remember are:

1) *In our solar system, there are 7 unique planes of consciousness that we move through on our journey of spiritual evolution*
2) *Each plane represents a unique field of existence just as real to its inhabitants as the Physical Plane is to us*
3) *The Physical Plane that we know best, is the lowest of the 7 planes*

Bringing it down to earth

Getting back to our lives here on earth, let's take a look at how this new understanding of the structure of the universe affects what happens to each of us after death. To do this, let's begin by looking at an image that explains some of the details about the 7 planes of consciousness in our solar system.

The 7 Planes of Consciousness

1) Divine Plane – home of the Source of our existence	
2) Monadic Plane – home of the Monads (our individual spirits which are fragments of the Source)	
3) Spiritual Plane – home of *Will* power	
4) Intuitional Plane – home of *Wisdom/Love*	
5) Thought Plane – home of *Intellect*	1) Upper
(3rd Heaven)	2) thought
Sub-planes of abstract thought	3) sub-planes
Sub-planes of concrete thought	4) Lower
(2nd Heaven)	5) thought
	6) sub-
	7) planes
6) Astral Plane – emotional realm	1) Upper
Summer Land (1st Heaven)	2) astral
	3) sub-planes
	4) Middle
	5) astral
	6) sub-planes
	7) Underworld
7) Physical Plane - physical existence	1) Atomic
	2) Sub-atomic
Etheric sub-planes	3) Super-etheric
(carry forces that sustain all visible life)	4) Etheric
Material sub-planes (world that we perceive)	5) Gas
	6) Liquid
	7) Solid

The Physical Plane, the plane with which we are all familiar, **represents the lowest level of consciousness** that humanity is moving through on its path of spiritual evolution. It is called plane number 7 (*numbering from the top downward*). Notice that the *Physical Plane* is divided into 7 sub-planes: 3 we are familiar with (the solids, liquids and gasses) and 4 higher states of matter that are unknown to mainstream science, and that have been given the name "etheric" (after the word "ether", which indicates a very thin, invisible substance). Although this etheric matter is invisible, it is absolutely necessary to preserving life as we know it. For example, our physical bodies have an etheric counterpart – called the *etheric double* – that serves as a channel for the life forces that maintain all the functions of the human body. Without the etheric double and the life forces that it carries, our physical bodies would simply drop dead.

And even though the existence of this finer physical matter is still a mystery to many, science is on the verge of discovering it; and when it does, health care as we know it will be revolutionized. (*More details about the etheric double and how it impacts our experience of death will be given in Chapter 4.*)

Plane number 6, called **the Astral Plane, represents a realm comprised of desires and emotions**. This is a plane we all pass through after death. It also has seven sub-planes that are divided into 3 main groupings: The lowest, middle, and upper astral. The experiences that people have after death on these different groupings of sub-planes are *very* different from one another (*and will be described in detail in Chapter 5*). For now, we should simply note that the lowest sub-plane is known as the underworld since it lies mostly beneath the planet; the middle three astral sub-planes are in close connection with the earth as we know it; and the upper three sub-planes contains a happy realm created by group desires sometimes called the "Summer Land" or 1st heaven.

Plane number 5, the ***Thought Plane, is – just as its name implies – a realm made up entirely of thought creations*** (and just as real to its inhabitants as our Physical Plane is to us). This plane, too, has 7 sub-planes. But in this case they are divided into 2 large groupings. The lower 4 sub-planes of the Thought Plane contain the realm of *concrete thought* or 2nd Heaven, and it features a life so beautiful and magnificent that it compares with our highest conceptions of the traditional Heaven – full of happiness, bliss and love. But this is not a place that we "go for all eternity". Our stay in this realm only lasts a fixed amount of time (which varies based on the quantity of unselfish thought we had in life) before we move on to the highest 3 sub-planes, the realm of *abstract thought* or 3rd Heaven. This highest part of the thought world is home to a transcendent existence beyond all words to describe. It is also home to the lowest manifestation of the human soul, the relatively permanent part of us that persists through all the lives we take on earth. And because we are now at the level of the soul, we are able to see our past lives laid out before us, along with all the lessons we learned in our earth school during our past lives, along with the lessons we still need to learn before we are allowed to break free from the wheel of rebirth (*more details on the Thought Plane will be covered in chapter 6*).

When it comes to planes 1 through 4, we need not concern ourselves with them at this point since the current field of human evolution is taking place within planes 5, 6 & 7. ***What can be said about planes 1-4 is that they are non-physical realms of consciousness that represent vast fields of evolution for innumerable forms of life that work with stupendous spiritual forces that help build and sustain life.*** We also know that these 4 highest planes are realms of unity consciousness; and as we rise through planes 4 through 1, we feel more and more as if we are part of *All That Is* rather than separated and isolated individuals. At these heights, we no longer look upon another soul as being outside of ourselves; instead, we experience them from the *inside*, and feel their experiences as if they were our own. Yet through all this strange change in perspective, we are not absorbed into the *Source,* only to lose our hard-earned individual consciousness. Instead, we retain all our memories of the past individual lives we lived – and still feel just as much our old selves – except now we somehow feel that the infinite consciousness of the *Source* has been poured into us!

Closer to home, we know a great deal through direct investigation of planes 7, 6, and 5. And there is more than enough for us to learn about the *Physical, Astral* and *Thought Planes* and how they impact our lives on the other side after death.

One thing to bear in mind when thinking about these planes of consciousness is that they aren't stacked one on top of another like the shelves of a bookcase (*although this is the easiest way for us to understand and study them*). In reality, they all interpenetrate one another so that we have all seven planes here on the surface of the earth. (*Though it is also true that the higher planes extend farther away from the earth's surface*). So, if we wanted to move from the *Physical* to the *Astral Plane*, we wouldn't have to make any movement in space. Instead we would just shift our consciousness from one plane to the other and we would become conscious of a whole new world all around us.

How and why the 7 planes come into being

In order to understand the formation of the 7 planes, we first need to take a quick detour into the basic concepts surrounding "how?" and "why?" the universe came into existence.

This is going to take a big leap of imagination – and it's going to be mind-blowing – but let's give it a try.

The first thing to understand is that life is much fuller and grander than most of us have been taught. For starters, we are going to have to propose a *Creative Force* that brought all the perfection and beauty we see around us into existence, holds it in various forms for the purpose of evolution, and then dissolves forms that have served their purpose only to create again. If you have a scientific mind like me, you might be a little uncomfortable with this notion. But for our purposes, let's throw away all negative ideas surrounding personal deities and instead consider a Force that represents the highest level of consciousness imaginable. ***Whatever idea of all-encompassing love, power and intelligence makes sense to you, just use that conception.***

Now getting back to our journey through the formation of the universe, let's take a look at the teaching of the Wisdom Tradition regarding this topic.

The Absolute

The members of the Great White Lodge that guide our evolution tell us about stupendous cosmic planes of existence far beyond the 7 planes of consciousness we are familiar with. And further still, above and beyond them all, existing in an unmanifested state, rests the Absolute over all. Anything we could say about the Absolute would express a limitation, which would be incorrect. The best way to imagine the Absolute is summed up in the idea of *Boundless Being*; and the *Root of All Existence*. ***From the Absolute spring forth an infinite number of universes, of which our universe is only one!***

The Universal Being

When it comes to considering the one universe we live in, we have been taught that it is brought into existence by a fragment of consciousness from the Absolute. This fragment, called The Universal Being, gave birth to the estimated 2 trillion galaxies in our visible universe – each containing an average of about 100 billion stars – plus many other realms and worlds of existence that we cannot observe with physical instruments. (*And, as we already know, the visible portion of the universe makes up only about 5% of what is really there!!!*) Our entire universe, both the seen and the unseen portions, is held *within* the Universal Being. There is nothing in our universe that is not a part of this grand consciousness which sustains all life.

The Solar Deity or Logos – the creator of our solar system

On a level a little closer to home, we are also taught that each and every star in the sky, including our own sun, is the physical manifestation of a Great Spiritual Being that lies behind. This Great Being has a life and evolution of its own and is literally one of the offspring of The Universal Being. The Great Being who gave birth to *our* solar system is referred to as the Solar Deity or the Logos. (The term logos is Greek and means, "*the word*"; which refers to creation being brought about by the spoken word. *Of course, this doesn't mean "speaking" as we know it. This terminology is symbolic and refers to matter of all 7 planes of our solar system being brought into existence through rhythmic, orderly vibration on a scale beyond our ability to fully comprehend*)

It is the Logos of our system that has all the power, love and intelligence that we can imagine in our highest conception of a personal deity. And ***it is the Logos of our system <u>in whom</u> we live and move and have our being.*** (*there is no such thing as being separate from the Logos, the Source of our lives. Everything around* *us – people, animals, plants, the earth, the air, and the so-called "space" between the planets – is held <u>within</u> the body of our Solar Logos*)

Therefore, when people talk about a Creator, it is important to be clear whether we are referring to the Absolute, The Universal Being, or the Logos of our solar system.

To summarize for easy reference:

The Absolute – The ONE, the Unmanifest. The Absolute rests behind all existence and gives birth to innumerable universes.

The Universal Being – came forth from the Absolute and created all the billions of galaxies and innumerable stars and planets in our universe.

The Solar Deity or Logos – the creator of our solar system. Every star in our universe is a Solar Deity that gave birth to its own solar system.

We are not alone in the universe

The Wisdom Tradition also tells us that each and every solar system is teeming with multiple and diverse forms of conscious life; some of which we would recognize as physical life, and other non-physical forms of consciousness that exist on higher planes. Either way, **there is no such thing as "dead matter", and there is absolutely no such thing as a single star in the sky that does not have life associated with it in one form or another. In fact, THERE IS NOTHING BUT LIFE, EVERYWHERE.**

The idea that we are alone in the universe is absolute non-sense promoted by those who would keep humanity living in isolation and fear. The reason for this should be obvious. When people are afraid, they are easier to control, and they'll go along with whatever those in power tell them to do. And the primary message we all receive is, "Just focus on physical reality and be a good consumer. Work hard and buy as much as you can", because that's good for business and profits. But the moment we realize we are creator beings on a magnificent journey of growth and discovery is the time we break free from our prison of limited thinking. Once this change in consciousness sinks in, life begins to take off in unimaginably beautiful ways. No longer are we helpless victims looking for external things to satisfy or save us. Instead, we realize that the earth is exactly what we have collectively made it. And the sooner we take responsibility for this creation and start working to improve it, the sooner we will see a new golden age dawn on the planet.

The evolution of consciousness

At this point, we are in a better position to understand the teaching that is given regarding the creation of the 7 planes in our solar system. And that teaching states that the 7 Planes of Consciousness are a necessary part of the evolution for our solar Logos. Let's take a closer look at how this happens.

In the beginning, before the creation of our solar system, we find that the Logos of our system picked a location within the Milky Way galaxy in which to create for the purpose of *Its* added experience and evolution (*just like we might pick a plot of land on which to build a home*). Once the location was determined, our Solar Logos enfolded within Its aura (*which can be imagined as a vast multi-dimensional sphere*) a tremendous area of space that stretched about halfway to the nearest stars. Next, a gigantic vortex was formed in order to draw all the pre-existing root matter scattered throughout space into the center of the vortex in order to form the sun and planets. At the same time, the Logos of our system created the 7 Planes of Consciousness by a stupendous effort of will; putting in motion all the atoms of one plane after another over great eons of time, starting with the highest plane and working step by step all the way down to the Physical Plane we know best. ***And this whole system of 7 planes is designed to offer the ideal environment for the evolution of spiritual life through an almost infinite variety of experience.***

Filling in a little more detail, the teaching of the Masters of Wisdom tells us that after the 7 planes were created, our Logos , threw off a part of itself - an enormous wave of spiritual life – which descended from the 1st or Divine Plane down to the 2nd or Monadic Plane.

This wave of life is just like its parent – it has all potential within it. But rather than creating perfect copies of Itself (*with no original creative expressions*) our Logos created spirits that started out as what may be imagined as "blank slates". These "blank slate" spirits were then destined to go forth and experience life for themselves and initiate new and original creations based on free will. That way, when each of the great waves of life returns to the Logos many eons in the future, they will bring with them unique and fresh ways of expressing life that will make them co-creators in the field of life.

> *As an analogy, we might best understand the reason for this by thinking about human relationships. Imagine if we had a partner that was created to be exactly like ourselves in every way. That might bring some harmonious living at first, but after a while life would become pretty dull! So, diversity of experience is crucial for mutual growth, learning*

*and sharing, both in our everyday lives, and even on
the Divine levels of existence.*

Evolution of the monad

Getting back to our life wave on the Monadic Plane, the first thing it did was to ensoul some of the most basic material of that plane (*atoms and molecules*). During this phase, the life wave, spent vast eons unconsciously evolving and learning to respond to all the vibrational opportunities at that level.

Then, once Monadic Plane experience was realized, the great life wave moved down to the Spiritual Plane and clothed itself in the atoms and molecules at that level to learn to respond to this lower level of vibrational combinations. Meanwhile, another great outpouring of life from the Logos moved down to the 2nd plane to take the place of the life wave that just left.

This process continues with wave after wave of life being thrown off by the Logos, and wave after wave of life moving down through the 7 planes until reaching the Physical Plane. This is the turning point. After experiencing life on the Physical Plane by evolving successively through the mineral, plant, animal and human kingdoms, the great life wave begins the long journey back up again, plane by plane; this time functioning in bodies made out of matter of each respective plane in order to learn to become conscious masters of life on those planes [It should always be kept in mind that life on the downward arch of evolution evolves unconsciously, whereas life on the upward journey evolves consciously]. Finally, the life wave returns to the Divine level carrying with it all the glorified spirits that are now co-creators in the infinite field of Life!

Each one of us is part of one of these great life waves and we are all engaged in a magnificent journey of <u>experiencing and</u>

becoming, *through an ongoing evolutionary process we call life and death.*

There is a lot of complexity to this evolutionary process I have intentionally left out. All we really need to keep in mind is that we are on the upward curve of spiritual evolution. We have already passed through eons of evolution on our journey down through the higher planes into densest physical matter. And now that we are in the physical world, we pass through many hundreds of lives until we learn the lessons of the Physical Plane. Once these lessons are learned, we no longer need to take birth in physical existence and our evolution continues at higher levels.

So, we should never think of ourselves as "less than". As human beings we are not perfect – and we all have many more lessons to learn – but *we are all "Sparks of the Divine Fire", destined to return to our parent fire to one day become as great as the One who gave us birth!*

The planes of thought, emotion and physical life

Now that we understand the basics about the method of spiritual evolution through the 7 planes of nature, we are going to focus on the lowest 3 planes – the planes of thought, emotion and physical life – since these planes make up the primary fields of human evolution at present. To help us visualize this, we are going to refer to our familiar chart of the planes of nature, except this time examining just the lowest 3 planes and the 3 "bodies" that we wear to experience life on those planes.

The 3 Planes of Current Evolution

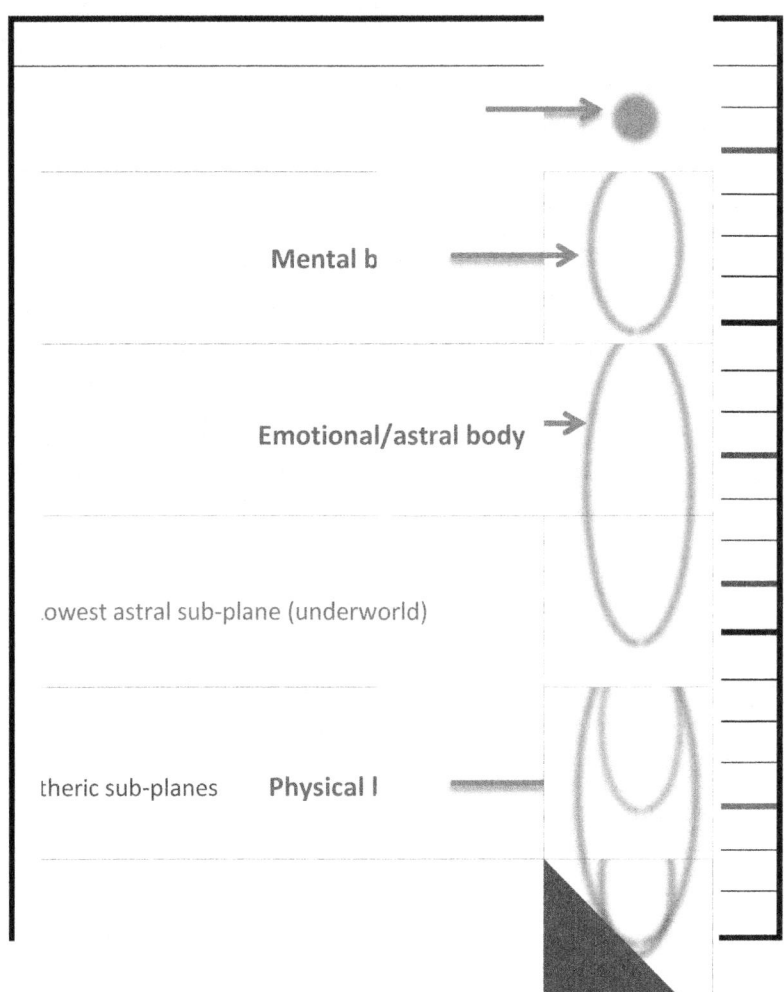

Mental b

Emotional/astral body

Lowest astral sub-plane (underworld)

Etheric sub-planes   **Physical I**

When the cycle of a human life ___ ndividual "Soul" that exists on the higher part of the Thought Plane moves down through the lower 4 thought sub-planes and takes on a body made of that matter (called the mental body; it then descends to the Astral Plane and takes on a body of that matter (called the emotional or astral body); and finally it descends to the Physical Plane to build the physical body. But when we get to the physical level, we find that the physical body is actually made of 2 distinct parts: the material body we are all familiar with, and something called the etheric double *("double" because it is an exact duplicate of the material body, although invisible to ordinary sight).* In fact, it would be more truthful to say the material body is a duplicate of the etheric double, because the etheric double is built first and serves as the mold for the building of the material body inside the womb of the mother. It is the etheric double that guides the process of cell differentiation and specialization that takes place as a fertilized egg slowly grows into a baby during the 9 months of pregnancy.

Since the idea of the etheric double is likely new to most people, it might be helpful to explain a little more about its role as part of our physical body. First of all, it is important to realize that the etheric double is not a hypothetical concept that someone invented because it sounds mysterious. It is a real object that can be seen by anyone possessing even the slightest degree of clairvoyance. It is most easily observed in dim light as a bluish-grey or violet-grey mist that extends about ¼ inch from the skin surrounding and interpenetrating the entire body. *The etheric double is made entirely of material from the top 4 sub-planes of our Physical Plane, and it carries the life forces that sustain and repair our dense material body.* These life forces – which have been called "chi" by the Chinese, and "prana" by the yogis in India, can be observed flowing around the etheric double along channels in the human nervous system.

Without the etheric double and its life sustaining forces (which guide assimilation of nutrients and oxygen as well as excretion of waste products) our material body would simply drop dead. There could be no existence as we know it without the etheric double. As we move throughout our day, the etheric double tries to keep our material body going by energizing the cells in the body.   But this process is a losing battle.   The mind and the emotions are constantly driving the material body to work or play. But eventually, when the etheric double can't keep up with the demands of physical activity, fatigue sets in.   Then, as we allow ourselves to sleep, the etheric double goes to work repairing the damage of the day so we can wake up refreshed to face another day. This is why sleep is so important for the maintenance of good health, and also why a good night's sleep is many times the best medicine for overcoming an illness.

The life forces and energy vampires

Another thing that might be of great interest to the reader is that the life forces that travel along the etheric double radiate outward once they fulfill their role in our bodies. When we are in good health, we radiate a tremendous flow of etheric force that helps protect us from disease germs. We can also direct the flow of this etheric force to other people by an act of will. We simply need to imagine the force flowing out of our hands to another person and that is exactly what happens. This is why *human touch - from well-intentioned and loving people - can help strengthen and heal another person*. This is also the motive force behind what is called Reiki.

A word of caution is also in order. Knowing the importance of etheric force, it should be obvious that we should not let people with "bad energy" touch us. Etheric force can be thought of as contagious. And if someone who lives a degraded, unhealthy or angry life comes near us or touches us, some of their etheric force gets transmitted in the process. This is why it is very important we carefully choose those we let near us: from our sexual partners and friends, to the people who cut our hair or even prepare and serve our food. And the best way to protect ourselves in these cases is to get to know people over time before letting them get too close.

There are also individuals in this world that can best be described as "energy vampires", who quite literally suck the etheric force out of the people they go near. Some of these "vampires" aren't aware of what they are doing and "feed" unconsciously, while others know exactly what they are doing and intentionally seek to steal the life force from others. We all know these people. After spending some time with them we mysteriously feel completely drained, tired, and sometimes depressed.

The best method for protecting yourself from energy vampires is to avoid them. There are times when this may be difficult – such as with a co-worker or a client – but if at all possible, limit your time with these individuals. Better yet, quit any interactions with these people as soon as you can, even if it means having to switch jobs or end a friendship or relationship. The main thing to note is that these invisible etheric forces are very real. And even if we can't see them, we can often feel them if we pay attention.

In summary, we need to keep in mind that *the physical body is not a simple thing but contains 2 parts: the dense material body we are all familiar with and the etheric double.* It is also important to remember that when we are born, we are a soul that is wearing 3 bodies; each designed to respond to vibrations from its own plane. For example, the mental body is the originator of all our thoughts and is capable of receiving and responding to thought on its own plane. Likewise the astral body is the originator of all of our emotions and is also receiving and responding to emotional currents on the Astral Plane. And the physical body – comprised of both the material body and the etheric double – receives and responds to physical vibrations from the Physical Plane.

Origin of thoughts and emotions

It is important to note that thoughts and emotions do not originate in the physical brain as scientists claim. Instead, thoughts and emotions are formed on the Thought and Astral Planes respectively and have to be vibrationally "stepped down" before they can be interpreted by the brain (*just like a high power electric current needs to be stepped down through transformers before it can be carried to our homes for regular use*).

The human brain is really just a 2-way transformer. It can take physical impressions and step them up to the astral body, which in turn steps them up to the mental body; and the mental body can form thoughts and transmit them down through the astral body (which adds emotion); and these thoughts, now clothed in emotions, are stepped down to the brain so we can take action on the Physical Plane.

The best way to understand all this is to remember that we are a soul; and that the soul is experiencing life on the 3 lower levels of existence (Thought Plane, Emotional Plane, and Physical Plane) through the 3 bodies we have (mental body, emotional body, and physical body).

If this whole system of "planes" and "bodies" sounds new and a little confusing, don't worry, that's normal. Consider re-reading the material and give it some time to sink in. Also, keep in mind that this system of different planes of consciousness was not invented because it sounds scientific, but because it has been confirmed by repeated observations made by trained clairvoyants. In fact, to a trained clairvoyant, we each look like a material body surrounded by several layers of colorful rotating mist shaped roughly like an egg. This has sometime been called the "auric egg" or the human aura. But this auric egg is a complex object and not just one thing.

For example, a trained clairvoyant looking at a person while focusing their attention on the Physical Plane would see the dense material body surrounded by the etheric double which extends about ¼ inch beyond the dense body. Then, as they shifted their consciousness to the Astral Plane, the material body would look slightly out of focus, but the astral body would now appear extending about 18" all around the physical body in roughly the shape of an egg (*and throughout that astral body would be swirling all kinds of colors that indicate the emotional state of the person observed*).

Next, if our trained clairvoyant were to focus their consciousness on the Thought Plane, the physical and astral bodies would appear out of focus, but the Mental Body, which also extends about 18" from the physical body in the shape of an egg, would come into focus (*and moving through this mental body would be a unique blend of colors that would indicate the persistent thoughts of the person under observation*).

The key take-away is that we are a soul that happens to be wearing several bodies in order to experience the complexity of life on the Thought, Astral and Physical Planes. And we take on these bodies for a certain period of time, and then leave them behind when their useful life is over; just as if we bought a car, used it for as long as we could, and then sent it to the scrap yard when it could no longer be repaired. The car's life is over, but the *car owner's* life continues. And this is exactly how the soul views its various bodies. These lower bodies are vehicles of experience that it uses as best it can - for as long as it can - to accomplish certain goals. Then, once the lessons of this life have been learned, the soul drops the vehicles, one after another until it returns to its own level of existence in the higher part of the Thought Plane.

The 3 great laws

Now that we know that our universe is made up of multiple planes of existence – and that our soul takes on multiple bodies in order to evolve through each of these planes – we are going to take a quick look at the three great laws that guide us along our path of spiritual evolution. And just like we need to understand the rules of the road before we drive, we also need to understand the rules of living in order to successfully navigate life! The funny thing is, most of us in the West have never heard about these laws unless we have been exposed to Eastern teachings. *It is as if we were all given cars without ever needing to go through driver's education. As a result, most of us have been travelling through life causing all kinds of wreckage for ourselves and for others without really understanding why there is so much unhappiness and confusion in the world!*

So, this section is quite literally our "driver's education"; our guidebook that will help us understand how to safely and effectively navigate life. And once we better understand the laws of our system, the smoother and happier our personal lives will become. Therefore, let's dive right in to the 3 laws:

1) The Law of Evolution
2) The Law of Rebirth
3) The Law of Karma (or Law of Cause and Effect)

The Law of Evolution

The law of evolution states that we are spiritual beings; and that the method of our growth requires evolving through many different forms - on multiple planes of existence - over vast eons of time until we learn to vibrate in sympathy with an almost infinite range of possibilities. Once we gain this vast amount of experience, we are destined to return to the Divine Plane and become co-creators in the endless fields of life.

To work effectively within this law simply requires us to recognize the fact we are spiritual beings having a human experience; and that the purpose of our time here is not to acquire money, property and prestige in order to indulge our egos and our senses, but instead to recognize our unity with all life, to be of service to the world, and to master a wide range of experiences across many different lives, in many different locations, during many points in history. Some of these experiences may be difficult, and others may be more pleasant; but the important thing to recognize is that *all the experiences we encounter in our lives are brought to us for a reason; and that reason is spiritual growth*.

From this point of view, we can begin to see that what we often think of as painful and difficult circumstances may actually teach us valuable lessons. Certainly, all of us can look back on tough times in life and realize that we came out better and stronger in the end, even though we didn't realize that something good would come of it.

The Law of Rebirth

Hand in hand with the Law of Evolution goes the Law of Rebirth. As we've just noted, *the method of our spiritual evolution involves taking on a multitude of bodies and forms over a vast number of lifetimes*, most of which are non-physical. In fact, the spiritual teaching we are given from the Masters of Wisdom tells us the average number of human incarnations is 777 before we are able to break the cycle of rebirth and move on to higher planes. Of course, this number is symbolic and there are some who take fewer births because they work harder to learn their lessons and others who take more births because they take their time and learn their lessons very slowly. But experiencing 800 lives on earth would be pretty typical for the average person.

For those who are skeptical about reincarnation, it is important to note that reincarnation is an observable fact that has been repeatedly witnessed by trained clairvoyants (and it can be confirmed by anyone who develops astral sight). But even if we have not yet developed the higher sight that allows us to observe the process of rebirth firsthand, we can quickly convince ourselves it is the only explanation for life that makes rational sense.

For example, how is it possible some people are born with the ability to rapidly develop amazing talents for art, music, speaking, organizing, learning languages, etc., even if their parents don't have such abilities? The answer is, these individuals earned their skills in previous lives and are carrying that expertise into their current incarnation. Without reincarnation, life is either reduced to the materialistic view (which states life is a cold series of random events that go nowhere) or the orthodox religious view (which claims life can be explained by an unfortunate game of dice in which "God" randomly assigns different talents and circumstances to people who are judged for all eternity based on what they achieve in one short lifetime). The materialistic view can be readily dismissed since everywhere science looks, they find order, beauty, mathematical perfection, and an invisible force that holds the whole universe together (which they call dark energy). And the orthodox religious notion would be cruel beyond all power of imagination, so we can cast it aside as being obviously false. Instead, *in this book, we are exploring the idea of a loving Creative Force that gives each of us free will in order to develop into intelligent co-creators in the universe through a slow process of spiritual evolution that is designed to make sure everyone succeeds*. And although some may get to the ultimate goal more slowly than others, we can rest assured that all will turn out well in the end since the system has been designed to bring each and every one of us to perfection!

The Law of Karma

The third law is called The Law of Karma (also known as the Law of Cause and Effect). This law works in a very simple way. If we put in motion certain *causes*, certain *effects* always follow. **The trick with the law of karma is to realize that all karma is not instantaneous.   The reason for the delay is to allow us the exercise of free will.** (Imagine if there were instant karma; then every poor choice we made would be immediately thrown back in our faces and our free will would no longer exist)

However, even with the delay between the causes and the effects, it eventually dawns upon us that **what we do to people, animals and the planet always comes back to us;** not always immediately – and not always in the same lifetime – but always and inevitably. This is the law of perfect and infinite justice. No one gets away with anything, even though to our limited vision it sometimes seems that way. Every thought, emotion and physical action that we have is recorded in the Memory of Nature and sooner or later bounces back to us. Whether quickly or slowly, our karma will always materialize when we least expect it.

But like all laws that operate in the universe, once we understand them and begin to work *with* them, they can be harnessed to make our lives immeasurably better. On the other hand, if we persist in working *against* them, then we bring down unnecessary suffering upon ourselves; not because we are being punished, but simply because we are working against Nature instead of with it.

Using the Law of Karma to our advantage

A perfect analogy that might help us understand how to work *with* the Laws of Nature instead of against them can be found by looking at a law we are all familiar with, the law of gravitation. One implication of the law of gravitation is it tells us that the earth pulls objects toward it at a certain rate. So, if I were on the 3rd floor of a building and wanted to get to the ground floor, I could jump out of the window (and probably break my legs) or I could take the stairs. Now, we might laugh at how ridiculous this sounds, but this simple analogy demonstrates the point we are considering. Since we understand the law of gravitation, we build stairs, or elevators, or airplanes if we want to overcome gravity without hurting ourselves. This is considered common sense and serves as an example of how we can work within one of Nature's laws without causing injury to ourselves or to others.

The same holds true with the law of karma. It tells us that what we do always comes back to us. But in our ignorance, we often do things that hurt others, hurt animals, or hurt the planet. This is especially true if we think no one is watching and we can get away with whatever it is we're doing. Or, worse yet, we do things to hurt the world around us because we are in a position of power and believe we are entitled to do what we want (like certain governments and large corporations).

Well, the Wisdom Tradition teaches us that **no one gets away with anything even though it may seem that way at the time**. Each one of us is accountable for all the karma we generate in the three worlds we are evolving through. In other words, <u>we are responsible for the results of all our thoughts, all our emotions and all our actions.</u>

This may sound stunning to some people since most of us think that if we don't hurt someone physically, we are doing no harm. And that even though we may harbor negative thoughts and emotions toward a certain individual, there is no harm done as long as it is not expressed. Well, that definitely is not the case. Negative thoughts and emotions *do* hurt the person that happens to be the victim of our wrath and these same negative thoughts and emotions also impact everyone nearby (*because thoughts and emotions – which can be seen by any trained clairvoyant – travel out from us just as if we were radio broadcasting towers*).   That's why being in the company of negative people is very damaging and draining because the thoughts and emotions of these people are contagious, spreading out in all directions to contaminate those unfortunate enough to be within range.

But sooner or later the results of negative thoughts, emotions and actions *do* come back to us.   For example, negative thoughts and emotions directed to others often come back as psychological and emotional disorders; while physical harm or hurt to others can come back in the form of physical distress, pain or loss.   The lesson here is that **selfish and negative actions, emotions and thoughts always lead to suffering and disease of some kind; while loving, selfless actions, emotions and thoughts always bring comfort, peace of mind, and happiness**.

Once we learn that selfish actions bring painful results, we will no longer make those choices and instead devote ourselves to selfless service to the world. And by following the path of service, we will increasingly begin to experience a life of joy, happiness and peace. This is a perfect example of how knowledge is power; and how using Nature's laws to our advantage can improve the quality of our lives. The Law of Karma is there to teach us that everything is inter-related and that there is a Unity behind all life. And this insight explains the true meaning of the phrase, "What goes around, comes around".

An example of the Law of Karma in action

We are now going to devote a brief section to the karma associated with harm to farmed animals because **animal slaughter is one of the biggest causes of <u>human</u> suffering on the planet**. This should come as a big surprise to anyone who is not familiar with how the Law of Karma functions; but by examining its workings in this specific example, it is hoped you will have a better understanding of exactly how this is possible. (*And, just to be clear, this discussion has nothing to do with moral judgments – or promoting vegetarianism*).

First, let's summarize what is currently going on in the meat industry because I'm certain very few people are aware of the situation. According to the USDA 2022 annual slaughter summary (which anyone can verify by Internet search), here are the number of land animals killed in the U.S. during a year:

Sheep	2 million
Cattle	34 million
Pigs	125 million
Turkeys	208 million
Chickens	9.5 billion

(Seafood is only reported by the pound; therefore, we are going to leave fish and shellfish out of this discussion).

Next let's consider how this is done. **Today, the vast majority of animals are raised on factory farms**. These farms are not really farms at all. There are no green pastures, wide-open spaces and happy smiling animals. Instead, thousands of animals are crowded into metal warehouses and spend their entire lives in cages and pens trapped in unhealthy conditions under artificial lights. (*Do a Google search on "factory farming" and look at the images for yourself*)

Factory farming is based on assembly line mass production technology applied to living beings; with the goal of maximizing profits through genetic engineering, the use of growth hormones, and regular doses of antibiotics to fight the diseases that animals get from living in overcrowded conditions. Of note, the U.S. Department of Agriculture started promoting industrialized animal farming systems in the 1960's, which helped drive down the cost of meat, thereby increasing demand. As a result of factory farming, coupled with a mobile middle class that was eating more fast food, the total per-person consumption of meat increased 85% during the 100-year period from 1919 through 2019 – rising from 150 pounds per person in 1919 to 278 pounds per person in 2019 (according to the USDA's Economic Research Service).

Now that we have a better understanding of the growing demand for meat, we need to return to the impact this has on animals housed in factory farms. Once animals reach the desired weight, they are loaded onto trucks and trains and shipped by the millions to mega-slaughterhouses hidden away in the Midwest to experience the fear and trauma associated with being "processed" on dis-assembly lines staffed by typically poor immigrant laborers.

Therefore, based on both the suffering occurring in factory farms as well as in the slaughterhouses, *we are faced with what amounts to an animal welfare disaster of unprecedented proportions happening right under our noses in our supposedly civilized society.*

[*For more information about the slaughter industry, consider reading Timothy Pachirat's book, Every Twelve Seconds. Tim is a Yale-educated PhD and Professor of political science whom I met at a conference on ending factory farming. He went undercover and worked in a large slaughterhouse in Nebraska. The title of his book refers to how fast the cattle were killed in his facility – one every twelve seconds – which works out to about half a million each year.*]

Given everything we've just covered regarding how our meat is produced on factory farms, let's take a look at the karma associated with this situation. We know from studying the Law of Karma that what we do to people, animals and the planet always comes back to us. Therefore, it should be easy to see that the massive amount of suffering, disease, anxiety, fear, and pre-mature death forced upon animals has no other outlet but to come back upon humanity. But the karma of the slaughter industry does not just fall on the owners of factory farms and the slaughterhouses, it also gets shared with consumers. And while most people are kept blind to the truth, we are still partially responsible because our purchases of meat, dairy, and egg products support this industry.

Most alarming of all, is that clairvoyant observation of the karma of meat-eating tells us that **one of the biggest causes of physical suffering, disease, anxiety, fear and violence in human society is the direct result of animal slaughter** (you may want to read this again). This is because the slaughter industry is so large – and the suffering is occurring on such a massive scale (globally) – that the result is what can best be described as a huge, dark cloud of negative energy continually pressing down upon the earth. And this cloud of negative energy actually impacts and influences all of us (*especially those more sensitive – like our children*); bringing back exactly what was done to animals into our own lives. Not as a punishment, but as the simple result of our actions.

I'm sure this will sound incredible and stunning to many people because we are used to looking to other sources for the cause of human ills. And although it *is* true that there are other causes of things like anxiety, fear, disease and violence, the important thing to realize is that one of the largest single sources of these troubles comes from today's cruel and unusual factory farming practices.

Easy steps to avoid the negative karma

Of course, the best option would be to move toward a plant-based diet. But if you don't want to stop eating meat, dairy and eggs, that's OK. Most people aren't ready to completely give up these products. Instead, consider buying meat, eggs and dairy products from sources that certify the animals were treated humanely. Or, if that's not practical based on budget or accessibility, consider simply eating less of these products by devoting a couple days each week to consuming entirely plant-based foods. And with the widely available plant-based burgers, sausages, chicken, eggs, and dairy-free ice cream, going plant based a few days a week is now super easy. Importantly, the taste, texture, nutritional profile (equivalent protein content), and appearance of these foods is now so good, most people won't be able to tell the difference; in fact, some may actually begin to prefer the plant-based alternatives because of their improved health profile (since they contain no cholesterol, hormones, antibiotics or potentially harmful disease germs that are always a concern in animal-based foods).

Using the Law of Karma to create the life of your dreams

On a more positive, uplifting note, we should realize that karma works both ways. Therefore, not only bad things come back to us, but good things as well (*In fact, for most of us, we have far more good karma in our lives than bad*). So, if we take a proactive approach to how we live our lives, **we can literally begin to create our futures by the actions we take today**.

For example, if you want wonderful relationships, start treating everyone you meet with respect, love and compassion (*this includes ourselves*). And, if you see someone else in a great relationship, support them and <u>sincerely</u> wish them well in thought, word, and deed.

If you want physical abundance (*enough money to afford a clean, decent place to live*) then start helping others less fortunate than yourself achieve the same thing. (*This doesn't mean we have to give money. It is actually far better for us to give of ourselves by doing things like: volunteering to help the homeless; supporting food drives in our communities; pitching in for a neighborhood cleanup;*

building affordable housing; helping others succeed at their jobs; or making sure anyone that works for us is fairly compensated)

This may sound simplistic, but it works! <u>Nature has no choice but to give back to us what we put out there.</u> Therefore, ***each and every one of us has the power to create the life of our dreams by giving away what we want.*** This is the Law of Karma in action; why not use it to your advantage? And the sooner you start, the sooner you will begin to enjoy a better life.

Summary of the 3 laws

Pulling all 3 of the great laws together – The Law of Evolution, The Law of Rebirth, and The Law of Karma – we are now in a better position to realize that:

We are spiritual beings, evolving through many lifetimes of experience, on many different planes of existence, operating under the law of karma.

And the sooner we recognize the Unity behind all life - and acknowledge that what we do <u>always</u> comes back to us - the sooner we will find peace, happiness and fulfillment because we will be working *with* the great Divine plan for our development instead of against it.

The Meaning of Life

and Death

∞ **Chapter 2** ∞

The Meaning of Life

Life as our "school" of experience

Now that we have a better sense of who we really are (*a soul wearing multiple bodies*), and how life operates (*under the 3 great laws of evolution, rebirth and karma*), we are in a better position to understand the purpose and meaning of life.

First of all, our definition of the term "life" needs a complete overhaul! Since we now know that every one of us is immortal, we can begin to understand that *our true life is continuous.* All that changes is the plane of nature on which our consciousness happens to be focused at a certain point in time. So, ***what we currently call "life" is simply the period of time that our consciousness is focused on the Physical Plane. And what we call "death" is the dropping of our physical body and the transfer of our consciousness to the Astral Plane to live in our astral body.***

Given this new understanding of our true immortal natures, we now have a better perspective on what everyone calls "life"; which we will refer to as *physical life* from this point forward. Therefore, the aim of this section will be to give an outline of the purpose and meaning of *physical life* in this *physical world*.

The best way to understand the purpose and meaning of physical life is to look at it from the perspective of the soul. From that higher point of view, the descent into physical life is necessary to learn all the lessons that the physical world has to teach. Since we observed in Chapter 1 that the method of spiritual growth is for each of us to descend through all the planes of nature and then rise back again to the highest plane as perfected children of the Divine, we can imagine that we will need to spend vast amounts of time on each of the planes in order to master the various vibrational experiences they have to offer. Knowing this, it's obvious that one physical lifetime on earth could never teach us all that the Physical Plane has to offer. And by now it should also be obvious that it will require <u>many</u> physical lives to learn the lessons of the Physical Plane. In fact, *for most souls it will take around 800 lives*, as was mentioned in the last chapter.

From this higher perspective we can see that what we call physical life is really just one day at school for our soul. **We come into physical existence to learn our lessons. Some of them we do well, and others we don't do so well. Then, after death, we learn from both our successes and our mistakes, and begin to prepare for another birth in order to pick up our lessons where we left off.** At first the lessons are very basic as we take birth in a series of lives in primitive cultures in a variety of locations around the world to learn things like survival skills, taking care of the body, reproduction, farming, etc. Later in our "schooling" we graduate to higher "grades" and move on to more advanced lessons. And these more advanced lessons might require us to take birth in a series of lives in more developed cultures to learn about cooperation, government, treating other nations with respect, planning for the future, acquiring property, or taking on positions of responsibility. And in the final stage of our physical lives on earth, we may take birth in more peaceful, enlightened parts of the planet to learn lessons about building community, creating art and music, developing high spirituality, and practicing the virtue of sharing and giving.

Of course, there is no fixed pattern for how lives need to unfold. But the general method is to take birth first in more primitive societies and later progress to more advanced ones; all the while experiencing different parts of the earth during different periods in history. And, in order to gain the full range of experiences available, we take both male and female incarnations within different racial groups; though choice of gender is a matter of free will and there are some souls that prefer to take birth in one sex more frequently than another.

Now you are officially an expert in the purpose and meaning of life; which is to gain experience! Recognizing this, we can see at once the impossibility of the definition that we have been sold, which claims that the purpose of life is happiness. It should be obvious that such an idea is a hedonistic and materialistic point of view. And, as we now know, simply not true. But this doesn't mean that we have to immediately go to the other extreme and say that all life is suffering, which is just a false interpretation of some of the teachings in Buddhism.

Here's where the confusion comes in: It is obvious that things like war or famine cause suffering, but those are always temporary conditions, even if they do last for a number of years. On the other hand, _long-lasting human suffering comes from unfulfilled desires_; wanting things that we think we need in order to be happy. The trouble is, more is never enough. And once we have something, we immediately begin to fear its loss or start to crave something else. *This cycle of wanting more and worrying about losing what we have is based on fear.* And this constant wanting and worrying about our desires is the cause of life's ongoing suffering. But the way to break the cycle is simple; though it takes hard work and a lot of practice. So, let's take a look.

The secret to a happy life

The secret to true happiness lies in being content with what we have. This does not mean we just lie around and stop working to build better lives for ourselves, our loved ones, and the world around us; but it does mean letting go of the constant desire for *more* and giving thanks for everything we have.

A simple way to break the cycle of desire is to do a gratitude list every day. Just take out a scrap of paper and write down everything you are grateful for. Keep it simple. Include things like a roof over your head, a job, food, hot running water, friends, a pet, etc. After doing this a few times you will find that *it changes your perspective on life.* More and more you will start to become happy with the little things that are often taken for granted every day. And eventually you may wish to get in the habit of doing a gratitude list in your head. Anytime you feel unhappy, just pause and run through your gratitude list. Without fail, you will start to feel better, even in the midst of *seeming* bad circumstances. Just ask anyone who has been through some difficult trials in life. Something good always comes out of these experiences, even though we might not realize it until much later.

Therefore, always keep in mind that our lives are about the experiences we gain while in the physical world. This should give us a much healthier perspective on the challenges of life. Instead of grumbling, complaining and crying, we can now say to ourselves, *"There must be some lesson I need to learn here. Let me figure out what that lesson is so I don't have to repeat it again!"* And once our lessons are learned, they drop away and we are free to move on to new lessons and new adventures in life.

Life on the other side during sleep

Now we are going to move on to another aspect of our physical lives that is mostly overlooked and completely misunderstood by the majority of people (including scientists) and that is our time spent in sleep. Most of us have been told that sleep is just a time for the rest of our physical bodies and that dreams are just jumbled up fragments of memories floating through our brains. Well, these ideas are only partially true. The Wisdom Tradition tells us that the physical body does indeed need to rest at night, but that we actually live another life at night, just as real as the life we lead on the Physical Plane. Let's take a look.

It may be surprising to learn that *each and every one of us leaves our bodies at night and travels around the Astral Plane.* Sleep is a time for rejuvenation and repair of the physical body, and that repair takes place at night when the dense material part of our physical body is finally at rest and the etheric double is able to do the work of repair (*that's its purpose*). All during waking life, the etheric double is energizing and supporting the physical body. But mind and desire nature constantly drive the body to work, move, think and experience. Over time, all this activity causes the physical body to exhaust more energy than the etheric double can replace. Eventually the body becomes tired, and sleep follows. Once this happens, the astral and mental vehicles withdraw themselves from their physical counterparts, and we have the spectacle of the soul, clothed in the mental and astral bodies, free to move about the Astral Plane.

Yet when we travel around in the astral body, we never have to worry about getting lost and not being able to find our way back because the astral vehicle is always tied to the physical body by what is called the *silver cord*; a semi-permanent link that ties the physical and astral bodies together until death severs the cord and the higher vehicles leave the physical body behind for good.

This is why many people who have near-death experiences can come back to life after visiting the other side. They may leave the physical body because of some trauma – say a heart attack or drowning – and they move about the Astral Plane in their astral bodies, sometimes observing the people who are trying to revive the physical body, and other times traveling to parts of the upper Astral Plane through the familiar "tunnel of light" to have certain experiences that usually tell them it is not their time. Regardless of what happens to these people, their silver chord is *still attached* to their physical bodies, otherwise they would truly be dead and could not be revived. (*Plus, there is no limit to where we can go on earth while traveling with the silver cord attached. In fact, we can move throughout earth's Astral Plane to any distance and still return safely to our physical body*).

Traveling in our astral bodies

In order to effectively use the astral body, it has to be developed as a vehicle of consciousness through practice - just like an infant has to practice using a new physical body. At this point in human evolution, we find that most people who have many previous lives behind them usually have their astral bodies fully developed as vehicles of consciousness; and are therefore free to move about the Astral Plane at night. However, **many of us are a little shy about using the astral body and are not quite sure about its powers (for example, being able to fly or pass right through what appears to be "solid" physical objects without being hurt).** As a result of this hesitation, we may move about very little on the Astral Plane; not going too far from the physical body, or even just floating nearby in a dreamy state thinking over the events of the last day while paying little attention to all the activity around us.

The idea of a nightly life on the Astral Plane is usually new information for the vast majority of people and will likely sound unbelievable. The reason for this is because most of us have no memory of these events and therefore we think they must not be taking place. Well, that is simply not true. The fact that we don't remember our travels in the astral world does not mean they haven't happened, and there is a logical explanation for it.

The lack of memory of these experiences results from a protective layering around the physical body called the etheric web. This web is made up of the atomic matter of the highest sub-plane of the Physical Plane (*sub-plane #1 listed on our familiar chart of the 7 planes*). It is a highly compressed network of atoms that are there to protect us from all kinds of influences that would otherwise pour in from the lower Astral Plane – many of them of a very unpleasant nature. ***The etheric web is quite literally like a suit of armor that protects us from negative influences from some of the less evolved "dead people" and other negative entities that exist in the lower astral world***. A rupture in this protective web would leave us open to obsession; which is just another way of saying that a discarnate astral entity could take possession of our physical body if the etheric web were damaged. *(Yes, this does really happen but fortunately it is very rare. The only way to tear the fabric of the etheric web is through events that cause extreme trauma – severe physical assault; uncontrolled emotional outbursts; extreme fright; and from heavy use of alcohol or drugs)*

The most important point to note is that the etheric web doesn't just keep out negative astral influences, it also blocks the memory of our travels on the Astral Plane at night. As our astral body passes through this web on its return to the physical body, it causes a temporary blankness and usually scrambles what we have seen on the astral plane with all kinds of fragments of memories from our waking life. And only someone who is trained on how to carefully carry their memories through this web can clearly and accurately report what they have seen on the other side. (*This is one reason why reports about what happens on the other side made by people who are untrained how to accurately bring through their memories may often be confused and biased. The other reason is that life on the Astral Plane is so completely different from our physical life that, even if someone could bring through a clear memory, it is highly unlikely they could correctly describe what they saw*)

Even though the etheric web blocks most memories of astral life, sometimes, little bits of memory *do* come through. Then we say we had a very lucid dream. But even these lucid dreams are usually hopelessly jumbled up fragments of what we have seen on the Astral Plane combined with all sorts of images and memories of events in our physical lives. However, when we have clear dreams of flying or floating without our feet touching the ground, these usually indicate experiences of astral life. And, sometimes, we may actually bring through memories of events on the Astral Plane that serve as pre-visions of events soon to happen.

Nightly conversations with the "dead"

An interesting fact about our travels during sleep is that we are able to meet and converse with anyone who has recently crossed over and still living on the Astral Plane. For these recently "dead" people, their time with the living is strangely reversed. They find they cannot communicate with the living during the times when the living are awake, because our consciousness is focused in our physical brains. But when we are asleep, and our astral bodies move onto the Astral Plane, they can have complete conversations with us. (7)

This fact should be reassuring to all those who have recently lost someone. *We can rest assured that each night after we go to sleep, we can visit with those we love on the other side.* But although we normally carry no memory of this time spent together into our waking consciousness, we may occasionally get a glimpse of this fact, and then we say we "dreamt" about them. Still other times we will awaken with a happy feeling or a sense of peace about a departed loved one, and that is a good indicator that we have met with them on the Astral Plane, even though we can't recall the details.

How to visit the dead at night

Even if you don't carry any memory of your visits with a loved one into your waking life, don't get discouraged. The visits will still be taking place. And with a few tips from the Wisdom Tradition, you can work at making these visits as helpful and productive as possible.

The best method for visiting someone on the Astral Plane at night is simply to set an intention for yourself to visit your loved one after you fall asleep. Write out this intention (along with anything you'd like to tell them) on a piece of paper and put it under your pillow. Lie down and keep the thought of your loved one - and what you want to say to them - constantly in your mind as you fall asleep. Then, as soon as you are fully asleep, your love for your departed friend will draw you together on the Astral Plane and you will stand next to them just like before. (*this technique works because love is one of the most powerful forces in the universe; and on the Astral Plane, the home of emotions, our friends will feel our love for them and will be immediately drawn to us*)

One final note. We should use the technique of communicating with the dead during sleep only for those who have recently crossed over. Life on the Astral Plane is limited, and most people will only spend the equivalent of about 1/3 of their physical lives there. (*For example, someone who lived 80 years on the Physical Plane would spend about 26 years on the Astral Plane; whereas someone who died at the age of 40 would only spend about 13 years there*). And out of that much shorter time on the Astral Plane, only a portion of those years will be spent in close touch with earth since the soul is all the time slowly rising through the astral sub-planes until that life, too, comes to an end and they move on to the transcendent life of the Thought Plane.

Plus, there is also a wide variation in the time spent on the Astral Plane based on individual circumstances. (*More about the astral life span and life on the Astral Plane will be presented in chapters 3 & 5*). But no matter what the circumstances, most people can be reached in our sleep for at least the first few years after they have crossed over; and that is the time that we who are still on earth usually need the most comfort. So, ***knowing that we can visit our loved ones during sleep has got to be one of the most reassuring thoughts we can have during our brief separation from them***; because one day, in the not-too-distant future, we will cross over and be reunited with our loved ones for the much longer and much more vivid life on the other side.

This is one of the most wonderful gifts that come from the teachings of the Wisdom Tradition regarding what really happens after death. With this higher perspective, you will find that death loses all of its darkness and terror. And in its place comes a quiet knowing and a sense of peace, born of the realization that none of us is ever really gone.

∞ Chapter 3 ∞

A New Definition of Death

Death as a transfer of consciousness

Now that we realize who we really are – immortal souls, taking on temporary bodies for each new lifetime – we can see that "death" is just the dropping of the physical vehicle so we can move on to the higher life of the Astral Plane. In fact, death is just the beginning of a continuous process in which the soul pulls further and further into itself, dropping body after body once the need for each vehicle comes to and end.

The sequence of death proceeds like this: First, at the end of physical life, we drop the material body along with the etheric double. At this point we are a soul wearing the mental and astral bodies living out our lives on the Astral Plane. And when astral life comes to an end, we also "die" to that plane and leave behind an astral corpse. We are now a soul covered only in the mental body living a considerable amount of time in the lower Thought Plane until that life also comes to an end and we drop the mental body and move into the true home of our soul in the higher parts of the Thought Plane. *Now you can see that we actually go through three "deaths" on our way to the home of our immortal soul on the higher levels of the Thought Plane!* To help understand this process it will be useful to divide this chapter into the 3 different stages or "deaths" that we move through on our way home to the soul, and then we'll explore the details of each of these stages in chapters 4, 5 & 6. To help clarify this process, you may wish to refer to the chart of *"The 3 Planes of Current Evolution"* located in chapter 1.

Stage 1 – Death of the material body

The first thing that happens when we begin to "die" to physical life is that the inner "bodies" leave the material body and hover nearby still attached by the silver cord. We now have the spectacle of our soul (the immortal part of ourselves) covered by 3 layers: the mental body, the emotional body and the etheric double (*which, as we know, is just a finer part of the physical body*). The etheric double is not meant to be a vehicle of consciousness like the other bodies, and it only persists for a short time after death. But while we are still encased in the etheric double an event of great importance takes place called the "life review". This is what people refer to when they say, "my life flashed before my eyes". (*details of the "life review" process will be explored in chapter 4*)

For most people, the life review lasts a relatively short time – from a few hours to 3 days. Then, once the soul has reviewed all the lessons of a particular earth life, it withdraws the sustaining life forces, leaves both the dense and etheric bodies behind, and the silver chord snaps. At this point, the body can no longer be revived, and the death of our physical body officially takes place. (*This withdrawal of the higher vehicles along with the severing of the silver chord can take place slowly – as when someone dies of old age – or quickly – like when someone dies of a heart attack or from a plane crash. But whether quickly or slowly, the process is fully understood by the soul when it happens. Therefore, no one dies an "unnatural" death. The main aspects of our lives – and our different potential exit points from life – are all seen ahead of time on the higher planes of existence as part of the lessons we have chosen.)*

We now come to the point in which the soul, covered only by the mental and astral bodies, slips into a brief moment of sleep and awakens to its new life on the Astral Plane. But as we can see by referring to our familiar diagram of the 3 lower planes of consciousness, the Astral Plane has 7 sub-planes that are divided into 3 main groups – the lowest (sub-plane 7), the middle (sub-planes 6, 5, and 4) and the upper (sub-planes 3, 2, and 1). And the experiences we have in these 3 regions are vastly different. We will explore the details of life on the different astral sub-planes in chapter 5, but for now it may help us to know that most people awaken to astral life in one of the middle sub-planes and slowly rise to the highest 3 sub-planes during their time there.

Once we reach the Astral Plane there is a whole life to be lived among our new astral surroundings; which are just as real to people in their astral bodies as are the material objects that we know in physical life. And in the astral life, just as in the physical, we can spend our time wisely or foolishly based on the choices we make (*because free will operates on the Astral Plane too!*). And just as we know of people on the Physical Plane that work hard and try to improve themselves – and others that accomplish very little and seem to drift through life with no real purpose apart from self-indulgence – the same holds true for astral life.

Stage 2 – *Death on the Astral Plane and the beginning of life on the Thought Plane*

Astral life proceeds, much like the physical life just ended, until our time there also comes to an end. And, **similar to what happens in physical life, there is also a "death" process on the Astral Plane. This is the 2nd death.** But there is no illness or pain associated with astral death. The astral body simply starts to fade away and life there begins to fade from view. Eventually, the soul drops the astral body, leaving behind an astral corpse to drift about and slowly disintegrate.

At this point our soul, clothed only in the mental body, moves fully conscious into a realm called "The Great Silence". This is a place of complete stillness and darkness. Everything fades away. We cannot think, yet we know that we are. There is a sense of being totally alone, yet without the slightest fear. At this time the soul experiences a tremendous feeling of peace; a peace beyond all words in which it realizes fully its connection with All That Is.

But our time in the "Great Silence" is brief. Soon after, an amazing transformation takes place. We feel a sense of movement towards a realm of increasing brightness. Then, our soul awakens to the exquisite sounds and sights of the lower Thought Plane; the realm of the traditional Heaven. In the upper astral sub-planes, where we experienced the joy of the "Summer Land", we thought life couldn't get much better. But as we awaken to life on the lower Thought Plane, a sense of joy and bliss overcome us that is out of all proportion greater than anything we experienced on lower levels.

On the Thought Plane, just as on the Astral Plane, we find there are 7 sub-planes. And they are divided into 2 groups. The lowest 4 sub-planes (realm of the traditional Heaven or 2nd Heaven) are where we go to live out our long lives in our mental bodies; while the upper 3 sub-planes (3rd Heaven) are the home of our relatively permanent "soul".

The lower 4 sub-planes of the Thought Plane represent a realm of pure unselfish love. And it is here that all the highest aspirations of our life just ended are realized. But this Heaven world is not a permanent place that we go to for all eternity. It is a temporary home, just like the astral life left behind. And we spend a longer or shorter time on the lower thought sub-planes based on the unselfish forces we set in motion in the life just ended. If we loved much, were truly unselfish, and tried to do our best for others, all these high aspirations find their *result* in the Heaven world. It is here that we get to experience all the love and unfulfilled dreams of helping others from the physical life recently ended that never came about because circumstances or limitations in our abilities prevented them from happening.

Here in the Heaven world, we get to realize these dreams and build the essence of all these high aspirations into qualities that our soul will store up as part of its permanent nature. It is here also that we begin to set the stage for the next physical life to come (*more details of the workings of life on the Thought Plane and the "Heaven world" will be found in chapter 6*).

Stage 3 – *Death on the lower Thought Plane and life of the Soul in its true home in the higher thought sub-planes*

Just as astral life came to an end, there is also an end to life in the Heaven world; and this is called the 3rd death. Once again, there is no pain associated with this 3rd death, just a slow fading away of consciousness on the lower thought sub-planes. At this point the soul drops its final covering, the mental body, and now stands free in its true home on the higher thought sub-planes to assimilate all that was learned in the physical life recently finished, and to plan everything it needs to learn in the next earth life.

The soul in its home world can be thought of as the relatively permanent part of us (although it, too, will pass away as the soul is transcended in a far distant future and the life of the immortal spirit begins on higher planes). The soul carries the memory of all past lives and knows the details of all the lessons we have learned. It also knows what additional qualities it needs to evolve in the future. Here, in the higher parts of the Thought Plane, the details of our next earth life are planned out; including the country, the parents, and the close relations that will provide the best opportunity to experience new lessons and work out the karmic ties we have made with other souls in the past. Then, once that work of planning for our next life is done, the soul begins its descent through the lower planes, taking on body after body (just like putting on multiple layers of gloves), until it finally takes birth on the physical plane to begin a new life.

Summary

To summarize what we have just learned about death, it's important to note that death is a continuous process of withdrawal in which the soul is moving inward toward itself; and in doing so, it discards 3 "bodies" in the course of time before it begins to plan for its next earth life. (**the physical body,** *composed of the material and etheric portions;* **the astral body;** *and* **the mental body**) Then the soul, free in its own world, plans its next life and takes on 3 new "bodies" on its descent back down to the Physical Plane.

At this point, a logical question might be, *"How long do we live on each of the planes after death?"* Well, the answer is, "It depends". The length of time we spend in each of our bodies varies depending on the life of the individual and their level of spiritual development, but a rough idea can be seen in the following chart:

"Life spans" for the bodies of the <u>average</u> person
(*Indicating how long our consciousness is enclosed in each of its vehicles*)

----

1) Physical body (75 to 90 years)

2) Astral/emotional body (typically, 1/3 of physical life; 25-30 years)
3) Mental body (from a few hundred to 1200+ years!)

Keep in mind that these are estimates based on the average person of today. There are many factors that can modify these averages. For example, we know that the life of the physical body can be shortened from accident or disease. But the other bodies (astral and mental) also persist for longer or shorter periods based on some very interesting factors.

For instance, a very materialistic, selfish or brutal person could spend a much longer time on the Astral Plane – say 50 to 100 years – and might only have a touch of experience on the Thought Plane before returning to earth. On the other hand, a really good and selfless person who lived a life of service to others might pass directly to the upper Astral Plane for a brief but joyful time in the Summerland, followed a prolonged blissful period upon the lower Thought Plane (or 2nd Heaven) that could last for 1200-1500 years. Still another exception to the usual process would be someone who died very young in life. In that case, they usually spend a short time on the Astral Plane and return quickly to earth, taking birth within a few years.

But the key thing to remember is that there is an overall principle at work: ***We take birth again and again to learn life lessons; and as our spiritual evolution progresses, and we become more and more unselfish, our time on the Astral Plane decreases, while our time on the Thought Plane increases.*** This process continues for many *hundreds* of lives for the average person until we learn all the lessons that are appointed for us in the school called physical life.

Then, as we approach a point in our development when our lives are increasingly dominated by high spiritual thoughts and service to others – a strange change takes place. We can actively choose to give up our long "Heaven" life and return to earth relatively quickly to take a series of births back to back to finish up our final lessons. (*It's like a runner in a long-distance race that is approaching the finish line and suddenly puts forth a great burst of energy and sprints all the way to the end*)

Once all our physical lessons have been learned, we then "break the wheel of rebirth" and no longer need to be reborn in the physical world. From this point forward we are free to carry on our spiritual evolution on the higher planes.

Of course, each of us has free will. And because of our choices, we can greatly increase or decrease the speed of our evolution (*and the number of lives we have to spend on earth*) by taking either the path of laziness and self-centeredness, or by taking the path of hard work and selfless service. But either way, the choice is ours. Earth is a "free will zone" and it is the soul that choses its own path.

In concluding this chapter it will be important to understand one additional fact: <u>there is no sudden change that takes place at death.</u> Because of this, ***many individuals wake up on the other side convinced they haven't died, simply because they are still conscious*** and still feel like the same "self" they were in physical life (minus a physical body)! The idea that life ends at death – or that, somehow, we are turned into angels or saints after death is simply not true – and has caused a lot of confusion for people when they first cross over. ***We live in a system of perfect justice ruled by the great Law of Karma. And because of this, we are exactly what we have made ourselves; both in this life and in the afterlife.*** (*Taking a common analogy, we can imagine that during earth life we are making our beds, and after death we have to lie in them.*)

In this case, as always, knowledge is power. And with a better grasp of the meaning of life and what happens after death, the more we can begin to live intelligently within our system of evolution. This means ***we can actively work toward building a better afterlife for ourselves by the choices we make today***. For example, by living a life of selfless service, we not only lengthen the more enjoyable part of our afterlife in the Heaven world, but we also set the stage for a more pleasant physical life in the future; all the while shortening the number of times we need to reincarnate on earth, and thereby setting ourselves free from the wheel of rebirth sooner than the average individual!

WHAT REALLY HAPPENS

ON THE OTHER SIDE

∞ Chapter 4 ∞

The Life Review

Learning our karmic lessons

With a basic understanding of the meaning of life and the process of death that we just covered in the previous chapters, we can now move on to a more detailed look at exactly what happens when we cross over. In this chapter, we are going to take up our afterlife journey at the point where physical death has just occurred, and the soul is hovering near our material body encased in the etheric double.

It is exactly at this point in the process of death that a period of great importance takes place, called the "life review". During the "life review" the soul sees the life just ended flash before its eyes *in reverse order*. This reverse order is intentional. It is designed to teach us about the workings of the great Law of Karma by showing us what particular *effects* resulted from certain *causes* that were set in motion earlier in the life.   To understand this better, let's take a look at 3 different examples:

> ***Scenario #1:*** Imagine the soul reviewing a scene from the life just ended in which its physical body, at age 89, was sick and dying in a hospice; but surrounded by loved ones and wonderful, caring medical professionals. Next, the soul sees a scene 20 years earlier in which it adopted a sick animal from a shelter, nursed it back to health, and gave it a loving home.

> ***Scenario #2:*** Now picture the soul viewing a scene in which it was cheated out of money at age 50. Then, immediately after, the soul recalls an event that happened at age 35 when it cheated a client out of money in a business deal by padding the hours required to complete a project.

> ***Scenario #3:*** Finally, let's imagine that the soul sees a scene at age 42 when it had miraculously found the home of its dreams in a quiet, park-like section of the city. Then, the soul sees a scene from its 20's when he or she was part of a volunteer corps that spent weekends cleaning up neglected neighborhoods and planting trees around the city.

By going through this process with life event after life event, the soul learns that *the Law of Karma is always in operation*, although many times we can't see its immediate results. Therefore, we can see from the life review process that we learn a very important lesson: **what we do to other people, to animals and to the planet always comes back to us!**

You'll note from the examples above that the most important part of the "life review" is realizing that nothing happens "by accident" and that we are all tied together. And even though it may take many lifetimes, it slowly begins to dawn on the evolving soul that **there is a Unity that underlies all existence.**

It is also important to note that each one of us gets to experience 3 separate life reviews when we cross over!

1) First, while we are encased in the etheric double, we see our lives flash before us in reverse order; seeing which effects were the results of previous causes. (*But at this point there is no feeling involved, just the observation of the workings of the Law of Cause and Effect*)

2) Later, when we move to the Astral Plane, we have another life review that also takes place in reverse order, except this time, since we are in the realm of emotions, we get to experience all the pain and suffering – and all the joy and happiness – that we caused others. In other words, we get to experience the results of our behavior from the perspective of those that we impacted (*this includes animals and the planet, too*)

3) Lastly, when we are planning for our next life in the higher part of the Thought Plane, we get to see the key events of our coming life in regular sequence from birth to death. At this stage, the soul is learning about what *causes* lead to specific *effects*. (*And, yes, we do get to plan out the key lessons and events of our next life; though we are still given free will as to whether we will learn those lessons. So, if an important lesson is not learned because of the poor choices we make, we simply have to come back in a future life and work at it again. For more on this topic see the books about*

life on the other side by Dr. Michael Newton in the Suggested Reading List)

It should be apparent at this point that learning the workings of the Law of Karma is an extremely important soul lesson. And by undergoing multiple life reviews in the afterlife, the methods of this great Law eventually become cemented into our soul's *conscience*. That way, when we come back to earth for our next life, *there will be some things we know that we just cannot do.*

Absolute necessity of silence after the death of a loved one

I'm sure we can see from what was just said, that the time immediately after death, when the soul is experiencing its life review, is of utmost importance. That's why there should be complete silence and respect paid to the newly dead during the first 3 days following death. ***Emotional outbursts – especially screaming and crying – are felt by our loved ones on the other side. And, what's worse, these emotional outbursts can actually interfere with the life review process because it draws the attention of the "dead" person back into touch with physical life in a most unpleasant manner and causes them acute suffering.***

The best plan is to send thoughts and prayers of good will and good cheer toward a newly departed loved one to help speed them on their journey. This way they can focus on the important lessons of their life review and find encouragement for a smooth transition to life on the Astral Plane.

Ghosts and the soul in the "grey world"

One more point will round out our discussion of the period when the soul is still enclosed in the etheric double, and that is its time in the "grey world". It is absolutely essential to our understanding of the etheric double to realize that it is not meant as a vehicle of consciousness (*It can be thought of as a sort of "bridge" of communication between the physical body and the astral body, but nothing more*). The result being that when we are still enclosed in our etheric double, we can't see events clearly in either the physical world or the astral world. Everything looks as if it were out of focus and with all the color bleached out. At this point the soul exists in what is called the "grey world"; neither "living", nor fully "dead".

Fortunately, this is only a temporary state of affairs (*lasting on average from a few hours to a few days while we experience the life review*). The number one thing to realize when it comes to our turn to cross over, is that there is nothing to fear. Instead, we should focus on the lessons in our life review, and then relax into a brief period of sleep while nature takes its course and our astral body shakes itself loose from the etheric double. For most people who die of old age, and for those who have lived a spiritual life, there is very little attraction to the physical plane, and so this process happens automatically and rapidly. But for those whose consciousness is still strongly anchored in the material world, there may be some difficulty shaking off the etheric double. These are people who either:

1) die in youth and have many attachments on the physical plane, or
2) have no thoughts beyond physical existence

As a result, these two classes of people often cling desperately to material life out of fear that their consciousness is about to be extinguished.

This is why knowing the facts about the after-death states can be of great help. Because when it comes to our turn to cross over, we can now understand that our brief time in the "grey world" is perfectly natural and a temporary state of affairs. We can also see that the best strategy is for us to relax and let nature take its course.

The worst thing that we can do is to fight this process out of fear. For example, people who are extremely materialistic and have no thoughts beyond physical life may become frightened and try to get back in touch with the physical world. Some of these individuals are so desperate that they often manage to hold onto their etheric double for months or even years, causing themselves much unnecessary suffering. They can even attempt to regain contact with the physical plane by attaching themselves to a weak person (obsession) or even an animal. Such attempts often fail, but there are occasions in which such individuals succeed and are able to see the world through the eyes of another.

However, most individuals in this sad state remain in the "grey world" roaming around in a sort of perpetual fog; forming a portion of what are called "earthbound" souls. They stay near earth out of fear of leaving physical life behind and sometimes make clumsy attempts to get in touch with others to make their presence known. Many times these entities are the ones responsible for noises and things moving around in "haunted" houses. *These are <u>one</u> form of "ghost", and they linger around their familiar earth settings, haunting these places until they finally let go and allow themselves to move onto the higher astral and mental worlds that await them.* (*The other common type of ghost are those individuals operating on the lowest levels of the Astral Plane, and we'll learn more about them in the next chapter.*)

The best thing we can do if we encounter earthbound souls is to send thoughts that encourage them to let go of earth life and move on to the higher levels of existence. Let them know there is nothing to fear, and that a higher and brighter life awaits them. All they need to do is relax and rest. Once this happens, the etheric double will begin to weaken and their astral body will shake itself loose and awaken to life on the Astral Plane.

The etheric corpse

Whether sooner or later, we all fall into a brief period of sleep after spending time in the etheric double. Once this happens, our astral body slips out and begins its higher and wider life on the Astral Plane. Meanwhile, the etheric double becomes another empty corpse, just like the material body left behind. And because of its intimate attachment with its counterpart, it tends to hover in the immediate vicinity of the material body, decaying synchronously with it.

But although the etheric double is invisible to most people, it is still comprised of physical matter. For that reason, any person who is even slightly clairvoyant can often see these bluish-white forms hovering over the newer graves in our cemeteries, reflecting the same amount of decay as the physical bodies below!

This is one of the reasons why cremation is highly recommended for disposing of the physical body after the 3-day waiting period is over. Not only is cremation a more sanitary method than embalming and better for the environment, it also releases all the physical particles back to their most basic state, and the etheric particles follow suit.

∞ Chapter 5 ∞

The Astral Plane

A higher vibrational existence in 4 dimensions

Now that the life review is over and we've moved on to the Astral Plane, most people must have questions like, "What does it feel like?"; "Is it just as real as living on earth"; "What would I see there?"; and "What kind of life would I live there?" Well, we are going to take a look at answers to all these questions and more in this chapter.

First we need to realize that the Astral Plane is not somewhere out in space. It is a large, multi-dimensional sphere that surrounds and interpenetrates our physical earth. And the "atmosphere" of our Astral Plane extends far beyond the physical atmosphere of the earth to about half the distance to the moon. (*We know this because the Astral Planes of the earth and the moon overlap when the moon's elliptical orbit takes it closest to earth, but not when the moon is farthest away*)

Plus, when using our astral consciousness we are now able to perceive a 4th dimension of space. (*Yes, the 4th dimension really* *exists, and, no, it most definitely is not time! It is an extension of all objects in a new direction at right angles to all the ones we know. The best way we can begin to understand it is to imagine moving <u>inward</u> while at the same time allowing our consciousness to expand outward. A seeming paradox, yet absolutely true!).* **The key thing to remember is: When we die, we stay close to the earth.**

When considering what it means to move into 4th dimensional existence, we can get some idea of all the new possibilities that await us by looking at a simple comparison between 2-dimensional and 3-dimensional existence, and then imagining by analogy how this can show us some of the possibilities of moving from the 3rd to the 4th dimension.

Starting out with 2 dimensions, we can remember from school that it is best pictured by thinking about a flat square (*length and width, but no height*). If someone were to live on the surface of that square, their life would be very constrained. For example, if a traveler living in 2-D space were to run into something blocking their way, they would have no choice but to go around. This would be like playing a game of checkers, but never being able to lift up one of the pieces to jump over another; instead we could only slide them side to side and forward or backward.

And we also know from school that no number of 2 dimensional squares could ever fill up a 3 dimensional cube, because the 2 dimensional squares have no height. Therefore, *we could fit an infinite number of 2-D squares inside of any given 3-D cube.*

If we now add a third dimension (*height*) to our imaginary life on the checkerboard, all kinds of new possibilities become available. When we come to an obstacle in our way, we can simply lift ourselves up into the 3rd dimension and hop over it. And while this may sound very simplistic, it gives us a perfect analogy, because we are now in a position to imagine what it means to move from the 3rd dimension into the 4th.

First of all, we can realize that **no number of 3-D objects can ever fill up 4-D space.** And on the Astral Plane, although it is full of life in every direction, there is no sense of crowding, thanks to the extra dimension. What's more, we also know from analogy that **things that used to present themselves as obstacles in our 3-D lives, like a locked safe, or a sealed Egyptian tomb would be very easy to enter since we would simply approach them from the 4th dimension.** So, when traveling in our astral world, there is no place on earth that can keep us out!

And with our new 4-dimensional perception, we will be able to see much more of everything around us. For example, when looking at a common object that we used to know in 3-D life, like a desk, we are able to see all sides of it at once (*as if we were looking at it from 6 different directions: from above, from below, from both sides, from the front and from behind*). What's more, 4-D sight allows us to see every particle that lies in the interior of the desk as if it were laid out right in front of us. But most surprising is that we also feel that we are simultaneously inside of each and every particle of the desk looking out at the world around it!

Our Astral Plane is also a higher vibrational plane of existence in which the particles are moving at rates faster than any physical particle known. And these fast-moving astral particles freely interpenetrate the physical world with great ease since astral matter is much smaller and finer than even a single physical atom. What's more, as some of us may have learned in science class or on TV, even the things that we call "solid matter", like rocks and steel, are mostly space. In fact, science tells us that each physical atom is spread far apart from its nearest neighbor – much like the stars in the sky – with vast spaces in between. So astral matter can easily move between and within physical matter. That's why both the Physical and Astral Planes exist right here on the surface of the earth. And the only reason we don't experience the astral world is because most of us lack the ability to "tune into" astral vibrations. (*But since we all possess an astral body, we* <u>*can*</u> *begin to perceive the astral world by learning to focus our consciousness within the astral body. We'll review more details on this topic in chapter 7*)

Just because the Astral Plane has matter so fine that we can't see it, let us not think that it is some imaginary realm far removed from the concrete reality of physical life. To its inhabitants, life is just as real as anything we know down here. And astral life is much like physical life; with vast collections of different kinds of beings living out their own lives. Some of these inhabitants are human; but most are non-human and include the lowest form of what in India are called the Devas (*equivalent to the angels of Christianity*). To quote from page 12 of C.W. Leadbeater's book *Astral Plane*:

> "So abundant and so manifold is this life of the Astral Plane that at first it is absolutely bewildering to the neophyte; and even for the more practiced investigator it is no easy task to attempt to classify and to catalogue it. If the explorer of some unknown tropical forest were asked not only to give a full account of the country through which he has passed, with accurate details of its vegetable and mineral productions, but also to state the genus and species of every one of the myriad insects, birds, beasts, and reptiles which he had seen, he might well shrink appalled at the magnitude of the undertaking. Yet even this affords no

parallel to the embarrassments of the psychic investigator, for in his case matters are further complicated, first by the difficulty of correctly translating from that plane to this the recollection of what he has seen, and secondly by the utter inadequacy of ordinary language to express much of what he has to report."

A great expansion of consciousness

For most people, the first thing that they feel when awakening to the Astral Plane is a tremendous expansion of consciousness coupled with a feeling of unbounded freedom and vitality. On the Astral Plane, there is no fatigue, no physical aches and pains, and no need for sleep since the astral body cannot be injured and it never gets tired. There is also no more hunger or thirst because our astral bodies get all the energy they need directly from the sun. <u>Can you imagine the freedom of no longer needing to worry about clothing, shelter, food, money, transportation or sleep?</u> For the first time in our lives, we can truly pursue our heart's desires without worrying about doing work many of us dislike just to support our physical survival. What's more, on the Astral Plane we can travel anywhere in the world with the power of thought because our astral body moves with amazing speed. Movement is not yet instantaneous – *that power belongs to a higher plane* – but it only takes a few minutes to fly from one side of the world to the other! (8)

How fast can the astral body fly?

If we take a rough estimate of the circumference of the earth as 25,000 miles – and note that the reports of investigators tell us it takes about 2 minutes to fly halfway around the world (12,500 miles) – that means the astral body moves at about 6,250 miles per minute, which is 375,000 miles an hour! Imagine traveling the 3,470 miles from New York to London in just over 30 seconds!

The Astral Plane is also a realm of *color*. The very essence of the substance that surrounds us is a form of brilliant living color that takes shape with amazing rapidity under every impulse of thought. (*In fact, the Astral Plane got its name from all the flashing lights and colors seen there; astral meaning "starry"*). On the Astral Plane, forms take shape, move around, and disappear with bewildering speed; all driven by the power of thought. The matter of the plane is instantly responsive to thought so, in the higher sub-planes of the Astral Plane that are removed from the earth, whatever we think about, we call into existence!

The 7 sub-planes

There are 7 sub-planes on the Astral Plane that can be grouped into 3 headings: the lowest, the middle, and the upper Astral Plane; and **our experience of astral life in each of the 3 groups of sub-planes is very different**. Let's take a look at a chart of the 7 sub-planes along with a couple of examples of life on those sub-planes so that we can see why this distinction is so important.

The Astral Plane and its 7 sub-planes

1) Upper	
2) astral	The "Summer Land"
3) sub-planes	(1st Heaven)
4) Middle	The world as we know it
5) astral	for background
6) sub-planes	
7) The underworld	

The first thing to realize is that **our lives on the Astral Plane are the direct result of how we lived in the physical life just ended.** The Astral Plane is a realm of self-centeredness, so whatever emotionally charged thoughts we had of a selfish nature, even if they involved loving thoughts of family and friends, play themselves out in the astral world. And depending on whether those selfish emotions were brutal, average, or of a higher variety directly influences the sub-plane we gravitate toward.

Do hell and purgatory really exist?

Let's get started with some really good news. ***There is no
such thing as hell.*** The idea of a place where people go for eternal
torment is a false teaching introduced by the medieval church in
order to control people through fear. However, the Astral Plane
can be pleasant for some, boring for others, or unpleasant for still
others depending on the type of life they lived on earth. So, in some
instances it *can* be stated that *there is such a thing as purgatory*,
which, as the name indicates, is a form of existence designed to
purge us of negative emotional states brought on by our own poor
choices in physical life.

But in all cases, whether good or bad, it is always a
temporary state, since the soul is all the time withdrawing further
into itself. And under the Law of Cause and Effect, finite causes can
only produce finite effects. (*In other words, we are only able to set
in motion a certain amount of force for good or for bad in our short
earth lives, so the results of those choices will be played out in an
equally limited astral life*)

**The main thing to get very clear in our minds is that
there is no such thing as reward or punishment. The entire
universe operates under perfect Divine Law.** And under the Law
of Karma we find that we are the makers of our own happiness or
suffering in the afterlife based on the choices we make during
physical life.

To understand this a little better, let's look at a few
examples of what happens on the Astral Plane as the result of 3
very different physical lives – the life of the brutal person, the life of
the average person, and the life of the more advanced individual.

1) The brutal, selfish person – this is a person consumed with
any one or more of the following: violence, lust, hatred, cruelty,
deception, extreme selfishness, powerful addictions – you get the

picture. Fortunately, most of humanity has evolved beyond this stage. But there are pockets of this behavior in some less evolved parts of the world, and even in the supposedly advanced Western nations. Surprisingly, this category is not just made up of "hardened criminals", but also includes those wealthy individuals, leaders of large corporations, heads of government, and people in the war industry that *intentionally hoard world resources, enslave and underpay millions, manipulate financial markets, charge usurious interest rates, and stir up conflict, all in order to profit from the mass of human suffering.* So let's see what happens to these people on the other side.

The Underworld (sub-plane 7)

Once a particularly brutal or selfish person dies and has their life review, they are drawn to the lowest sub-plane of the Astral Plane: the underworld. ***This is a region that lies somewhat on the surface of the earth, but mostly below it.*** This is not a fiction; this realm really exists. It is a place of darkness, fear and despair. ***Living there has been described as having a feeling of heaviness; like swimming through some thick, black fluid resembling dirty oil.*** In this world, people are acting out – over and over again – the same selfish and brutal actions they did in physical life. Except in this lowest astral sub-plane, none of their schemes ever come to pass because they have no physical bodies in which to realize their base desires. So, they go on repeating their actions but never achieving their goals and suffering tremendously in the process; all the while surrounded by the most indescribably loathsome creatures created by the lowest passions of humanity and beasts. (*Remember, thought is creative on the Astral Plane, so temporary creatures are called into existence by the thoughts of both people and animals on earth as well as individuals on the other side*)

But eventually these souls learn to let go of their lower desires, and once they do, they move up to higher sub-planes and begin a brighter afterlife.

> Side note: Because of its darkness and the unpleasant entities and circumstances encountered there, the lower astral realm is most certainly what the various religions have described as "hell". As we have just learned, there is no such place where souls go for eternal torture. However, while individuals are in the underworld, the suffering is very real and the circumstances of life in that realm most certainly make for an extremely horrific experience.

Although the lower astral sub-plane is very unpleasant, like all things in the astral world, it is only temporary. And anyone who is foolish enough to live a life that brings them into touch with this region is getting exactly what they deserve. Again, ***it is important to emphasize that the suffering in the lower astral world is not a punishment from without by some judgmental deity but comes from within and is the <u>natural result</u> of an individual's own choices in the physical life just ended.***

Yet, in the end, the suffering experienced in the lower astral realm is always turned to good. Nature is never vandalistic. Whenever an individual has to suffer because of his or her selfish and cruel choices, the soul learns a powerful and painful lesson. And this <u>experience</u> will be stamped into the higher memory of the soul so that in the next life it will seek to guide its new physical vehicle away from making the same mistakes. This is the source of the voice inside – our "conscience" – that tells us that there are some things that we just cannot do. Of course, we all have free will. And if we choose not to listen to that voice, we will simply have to suffer the consequences. However, as we know, any suffering is entirely of our own making; and the sooner we learn to treat others with kindness and compassion, the sooner will our suffering end and our lives become full of peace and joy.

> ***No worries:*** *the average person of today need have no fear of waking up on the lowest astral sub-plane after death. It is rare; and, as we have seen, the result of a brutal and selfish life. For the everyday person – even though we may make many mistakes – we don't have to worry about this fate. At worst we might wake up on the 6th sub-plane; still very much in touch with the earth and its trappings so we can learn to slowly let go of our attachments to material cravings as they burn themselves out from lack of realization. And once we let go of our earthly desires, we naturally rise to higher levels.*

Astral "Ghosts"

At this point it might be appropriate to mention a little bit about the other common type of ghost besides the soul in the "grey world" that we discussed in the last chapter. This second type of ghost is comprised of souls on the lowest sub-planes of the Astral Plane – sub-planes 6 and 7 – that are most closely in touch with the earth. As we just learned, souls living on sub-plane 7 are those who lived a brutal and selfish life. Sometimes these entities, instead of learning their lessons and giving up their low desires, seek to get back in touch with the earth and continue their evil ways. To do this requires a great deal of energy; and to get the energy they so desperately need, they look for the perfect energy source, the living.

In this case, human emotions provide the energy they need; the more violent the vibrations, the better. For this reason, swarms of lower astral entities can be seen by those with clairvoyant sight haunting places where extreme or degraded emotions are common; places with a concentration of fear, lust, cruelty, and hatred as well as places with abnormal amounts of excitement. Examples include battlefields, the sites of terrorist attacks, hospitals, prisons, funeral homes, slaughterhouses, sporting events, concert venues, movie theaters, bars, nightclubs, and houses of prostitution.

Lower astral entities – both human and non-human – feed off the emotion generated in these places, and they use that energy to maintain an abnormally long life on the lower Astral Plane. Once anchored in this position, they seek to influence the living in harmful ways in order to gain more energy by planting negative thoughts and suggestions in people's minds. These entities are often the source of the destructive thoughts that attack people who are feeling depressed or are on a downward spiral through addiction or a series of unfortunate events in life. And these lower astral entities are often the source of influence behind mass shootings and other events which generate large emotional outpourings.

These lower entities are attracted to people of similar taste, since "like attracts like" on the other side just as in this world. But such entities can have little effect on people who are living a good life. Therefore, the best protection from attack by lower astral entities is living a life of service and helpfulness to others. Once we do this, it's as if we put a shield around ourselves and any negative thoughts aimed our way simply bounce back to the sender. We can also imagine surrounding ourselves with white light during the day and before going to bed at night. This is a proven technique of protection that works for most people.

There are also souls living on sub-plane #6, which is closely connected with the earth, that form another part of the ghost population. Although these are not extremely brutal or selfish people, they are usually the ones who were very materialistic in life – knowing nothing of higher thoughts or emotions. These souls may move about the lower Astral Plane and also try to maintain contact with the living – and therefore "haunting" the places they choose to inhabit. They also feed off emotional energy and may frequent some of the same locations that were mentioned earlier. But these souls are not malicious and most of them grow tired of trying to continue their earth lives without a physical body in which to enjoy it. And when their thoughts finally turn to higher things in life, they move on to the higher astral sub-planes.

The best thing we can do if we think we have encountered one of these ghosts is to send them thoughts of love and encourage them to let go of earth life and move on to the higher levels of existence.

2) The average person – this group comprises the vast majority of people on the planet who are living a life in which they try to do what they think is good; but also make many mistakes along the way. These souls are not really bad in a ruthless or cruel sense, but they *do* have mostly selfish motives interspersed with a few glimpses of selflessness toward loved ones, which are usually just family and friends. These individuals have no special aspirations beyond the material life; being attracted to things like making money, gaining social position or power, shopping, and gossip.

People in this category usually gain consciousness on the Astral Plane for the first time in the middle Astral Plane (sub-planes 4, 5 or 6), which has the physical world as we know it for a background.

Middle astral sub-planes (sub-planes 4, 5 & 6)
In this region, people are still in touch with the life of the physical world just left behind. Many will still hang around places that they used to frequent in the life just ended and busy themselves living out their favorite activities. But without a

physical body, there are many of the old pleasures of life that they simply can't enjoy anymore; like food, drink and sex. For the gross materialist, life on these lower sub-planes will probably seem boring and time would weigh very heavy on their minds because none of the pretenses of the social life left behind matter any more. People are no longer hungry or thirsty, hot or cold, or worried about transportation; so, no one cares any more about money, titles, cars and houses!

In the astral world, language is still important, since we are not at the level yet where thoughts can be directly transferred (that happens on the Thought Plane). Therefore, *people on the Astral Plane tend to cluster together in groups with similar interests, languages, cultures and religions.* Level 6 of the astral world is the most closely attached to the earth. And people there go about trying to live the life just left behind until their desire for physical existence starts to burn itself out. As this happens, they rise to a new level (*a fact that is often reported by people who have been in touch with those who have crossed over*). And as they rise through levels 5, and then 4, the physical world starts to fade, and the desires of physical life start to fade as well. Once that process has finished, they are preparing to move to the next cluster of sub-planes, the upper Astral Plane, also known as *the Summer Land.*

3) The more advanced person – this class represents a steadily growing block of humanity as it moves toward a life of spirituality. They comprise those who lead lives of devotion to a higher purpose through things like music, art, science, family or society; although still mostly along selfish lines since they do these things out of pride, wanting to be recognized by others for how good they are and for what they have achieved.

Nevertheless, this group represents a large advance over the first two groups we just considered, and people that lead this kind of life generally move right to the upper astral sub-planes after death into the "Summer Land". *The Summer Land represents all the most beautiful longings of the human imagination, and contains breathtaking mountains, lakes and streams, dotted all over with magnificent villages, homes, schools and churches, whatever the people living there wish to create.*

The Summer Land or first Heaven (sub-planes 1, 2 & 3)

As in the lowest and middle astral sub-planes, like attracts like, so people of similar backgrounds, religions and languages group together and each group creates their own "Summer Land" with its own unique appearance and customs. For this reason, there are a large number of summer lands surrounding the planet; each hovering over a particular region and reflecting the language, customs, traditions, and tastes of the people who are drawn there; and all this without any sense of crowding due to the extra dimension in the astral plane. In this region, all that represents the earth that we know is left behind. The scenery is completely created by the thoughts of the inhabitants since everyone has the power to create whatever they desire. Most people who come to the Summer Land just accept the forms already created and may add a little touch of originality here or there to change the surroundings to suit their taste. For example, people can inhabit a home already built that isn't being used, or they could create a completely new one with the power of thought.

In the Summer Land we can expect to see landscapes and scenery that far surpass in beauty anything that the physical world has to offer. But if we were to think that a world created by thought would somehow be less "real" than physical life, we would be mistaken. *The creations in the Summer Land are just as real to its inhabitants as our landscapes and our cities are to us. In fact, since the Astral Plane is one level closer to the Divine Plane, its creations are one step closer to the Real Life.*

And because of its transcendent beauty compared to our physical earth, the "Summer Land" has sometimes been referred to as "the first Heaven". Though what most people would think of as "Heaven" - and infinitely more - can be found on the next plane up from the astral – the Thought Plane.

End of astral life

Eventually, just as on the Physical Plane, **life on the Astral Plane also comes to an end.** Our self-centered earthly desires, whether high or low, burn themselves out and the soul begins to withdraw inward again. We go through what is know as the "2nd death" and the astral body is dropped. But there is no pain, illness or period of unconsciousness associated with death here. Instead, the astral world slowly fades from view and the soul moves into a brief state of complete stillness and peace. All life that it knew fades away. The soul cannot think, but somehow it knows that it "is". This phase of the afterlife journey is called "the Great Silence". The soul stands alone in perfect stillness. But it feels no fear; only an overriding sense of limitless being. And soon after, a sense of movement takes place, and the soul finds itself passing into a realm of light while awakening to the breathtaking sights and sounds of the true Heaven world.

∞ **Chapter 6** ∞

"Heaven" and Reincarnation

The Thought Plane – home of the second and third Heavens

The Thought Plane, just like the Astral Plane, is not somewhere far off in space, but surrounds and interpenetrates our physical earth. It is a vast multi-dimensional sphere that extends well beyond the orbit of the moon, but it does not overlap the mental planes of any of our nearest planets (*Venus and Mars*). Here on the Thought Plane we are able to perceive a 5th dimension of space, and that opens up an almost infinite number of possibilities in new directions, similar to the expansion of possibilities we discussed in the previous chapter when looking at 4-D vs. 3-D life. For example, we know that any number of 4-D objects can never "fill up" 5-D space. And here in the 5th dimension we are faced with an amazing new form of perception. At this level, we are able to realize our "whole selves" simultaneously; that means the entire life just ended from birth to death is simultaneously present in our expanded 5th dimensional consciousness!

Additionally, if the Astral Plane was the plane of *color*, the Thought Plane can be conceived of as the plane of *sound*. There is still color, of course, but the sound is what pervades the plane and generates the color. Here sound underlies the vitality of all life.

When we first arrive on the Thought Plane, we live in our mental body on the lowest 4 sub-planes. This is the realm of the traditional Heaven (*sometimes referred to as the 2nd Heaven by those who consider the upper Astral Plane the 1st Heaven*). **This Heaven world is a place of inconceivable bliss. The feeling is one of boundless happiness and boundless being.** Let's take a look at a quote from CW Leadbeater's book, *The Devachanic Plane* that summarizes his investigations of life on the Thought Plane:

> *This intensity of bliss is the first great idea which must form a background to all our conceptions of the Heaven-life. It is not only that we are dealing with a world in which, by its very constitution, evil and sorrow are impossible; it is not only a world in which every creature is happy; the facts of the case go far beyond all that. It is a world in which every being must, from the very fact of his presence there, be enjoying the highest spiritual bliss of which he is capable — a world whose power of response to his aspirations is limited only by his capacity to aspire*

And since it is the realm of thought, whatever we think about, manifests instantly! Communication on this exalted level is perfect. There are no longer language barriers. Our thoughts take form in color and sound – which another person is able to perceive and understand – the meaning being perfectly clear. And here travel is instantaneous. No sooner than we think of a place then we are there, because **thought travels faster than the speed of light** (*the speed of light, as we know, is a physical limitation that has no meaning on the higher planes*).

Life on the Thought Plane can be divided into 2 large regions. The lower thought sub-planes (levels 4-7), and the upper thought sub-planes (levels 1-3). The lower thought sub-planes are the realm of <u>concrete thought</u> and the home of the traditional Heaven *(or second Heaven),* while the upper thought sub-planes are the realm of <u>abstract thought</u> *(or third Heaven)* and the home of our relatively permanent reincarnating soul. And ***the Soul functioning on the upper thought sub-planes has full memory of all the earth lives completed in the past.*** (*Therefore, if any of us gets flashes of memories of past lives, it's because a glimmer of consciousness from our Soul has made it all the way down into our physical brains*).

Thought Plane and its 7 Sub-planes

1) Upper	
2) thought	**Realm of abstract thought**
3) sub-planes	(3rd Heaven & home of the Soul)
4) Lower	
5) thought	**Realm of concrete thought**
6) sub-	(home of 2nd Heaven)
7) planes	

To understand the difference between the realms of concrete and abstract thought, it is easiest to look at some simple examples that will clarify this point.

For instance, the idea of a "house", or a "tree", or a "triangle", without any further details, would be considered ideas in the "abstract". But if we were to consider concrete ideas of the same items we would talk about "a white, 50-year-old ranch house in the Chicago suburbs"; or "a mature beech tree in central London"; or "an equilateral triangle measuring 3 inches on each side".

The Physical Plane we live in is full of concrete forms, and the lower Thought Plane is a realm in which the original concrete forms are *thought out* for everything we see down here in the physical world. Strange and new as this concept may sound, the Wisdom Tradition teaches us that **all of physical existence is just crystalized thought.** The thought comes first; then, the astral matter adds the emotion (or motivating force); and finally, physical matter gets molded into whatever we can imagine down here in our physical reality! (Of course, most of us cannot simply think of an object and materialize it into physical reality. We are not at a stage in human evolution in which people could be trusted with such power. But in the future, when everyone in society begins to operate from a place of love and selfless service, such materializations will become possible).

The Heaven life

Getting back to life on the lower thought sub-planes, here is a realm where all selfishness and lower desires have long ago melted away since they burned themselves out on the Astral Plane. Now is the time that we realize all our highest aspirations. Whatever unselfish thoughts we had – even though they may never have come into being on earth – will be played out to our delight in this world of thought. And **whatever friendships or loves that we** *had in our earth life just finished, we will find them here in a fuller measure than could ever be possible on the lower planes.* The reason for this fact is the Thought Plane is world of thought. Therefore, when we think about a loved one, we actually create what is called a "thought form" of them which looks exactly as we remember them. And the instant this "thought form" is made, the soul of that friend eagerly pours a portion of itself down to ensoul it and give it life. (*And since the soul exists in the upper portions of the Heaven world, no number of lower manifestations can ever exhaust its possibilities. In this way, each and every one of us can have our friends and family exactly as we remember them; but with a fullness of life more vivid and more real than anything we can experience in this limited physical world!*)

It is nearly impossible to put into words what life is like in this world of thought. Imagine the unbounded feelings of the happiest moments of childhood among our favorite friends and animals; amid oceans of sound and color beyond any human words to describe; and then multiply this feeling by a hundred. Even then we can only get a faint idea of what life is like there. All human concerns of the physical world pale into insignificance compared to the vivid life of the Heaven world.

And, as noted earlier, **this is not a permanent place that we go to after death as many religions have promoted**. The Heaven world is a temporary place in which we work out our highest aspirations and take the fruits of these experiences up to the soul. The Heaven world is also a place in which we plan our next life by reviewing the new lessons we need to learn and working on the environments and bodies that will be necessary to achieve our goals. Then, after we finish our long time of bliss and renewal in this region, there eventually comes a time when the soul withdraws its life force from the mental body and we die our 3rd death. And just like death on the Astral Plane, there is no pain or fear. We simply exhaust all that we needed to do in the Heaven world and the life of that realm slowly fades away. At this point, each of us awakens to a dazzling new life on the upper thought sub-planes.

The third Heaven - home of the soul

Although few of us have full consciousness on the sub-planes of abstract thought as yet, each of us will have at least a touch of this higher life, because here is the realm of the lowest manifestation of the reincarnating soul. Here, thoughts no longer take form when people communicate with each other as happened on the lower thought plane; instead, they travel like bolts of lightening from soul to soul, and entire lines of thought that might take many hours or even days to express in physical life are exchanged between souls in an instant. On these highest sub-planes we have full memory of all the earth lives we have lived in the past and all the lessons we have learned. Our soul also knows what skills it still needs to develop; so it plans out the next earth life considering the lessons that can best be learned during that incarnation. Then, once the new earth life is planned, the will to manifest on lower planes become irresistible and the process of descent into physical existence begins.

Reincarnation

Yes, reincarnation is a fact that has been verified by direct clairvoyant observation and by many examples of carefully investigated and verified reports of individuals who have experienced memories of past lives. (9) What's more, reincarnation is the only possibility that makes common sense if we really think about it. Let's consider the two main alternatives that most of us are familiar with:

1) The materialistic theory: blank nothingness after death

Does it really make sense that the entire universe and all of the tremendously complex and manifold forms of life that we know of are just the result of a random series of coincidences that followed the "big bang"? Can we really believe that all the experiences and learnings of a lifetime are just wasted, and that we just dissolve back into the dust from which we came?

Theory #1 is absolute nonsense. The idea that all the mathematical perfection and beauty of the universe is a coincidence can be disproven at once. Let's take a simple example to illustrate the point:

Imagine writing out several hundred musical notes of different tones and lengths onto small pieces of paper (one note per piece of paper) throwing them all into a shoe box and mixing them up thoroughly; then, running up to a rooftop and dumping out the box into the breeze expecting the notes to land on the ground arranged into a symphony! I think we would all laugh at this example and agree that this is ridiculous and impossible! But it proves the point.

When it comes to the infinite complexity of the innumerable pieces of the universe that have somehow arranged themselves into all the galaxies, stars, planets and myriad forms of life, we have an even greater impossibility of coincidence. Therefore, science has unwittingly proven the existence of a Guiding Force behind the creation of the universe long ago! It's just that the scientific establishment is stuck in its old ways of thinking and embarrassed to admit its mistake; though some of the more thoughtful members of this community are beginning to realize the truth. (*For example, the physicists who have proven that human thought is able to alter material reality. From here it is no stretch of the imagination to envision what the thought power of a Force infinitely more powerful than a human being could accomplish).*

2) The narrow "religious" theory: Judgment for all eternity based on one life

This suggestion is even worse than the last one. ***Does it really make sense that a God of infinite power, wisdom and love would create human beings as imperfect creatures and judge them for all eternity based on the actions of one lifetime?*** (even though one person should be born into favorable circumstances and another born into a life surrounded by crime and poverty?)

Of course not! That would be heartless and cruel beyond all imagination; and such a notion simply reflects a belief system based on fear and manipulation. The creators of this horrible lie knew that anyone who is *afraid* will do whatever the "powers that be" tell them they need to do in order to minimize their suffering and be "saved". In the past, those "powers that be" were the church and the state. Today, however, people instinctively know that there is something wrong with these fear-based teachings. And now, more than ever, we are looking for explanations of life that are in alignment with a Loving Presence in the universe.

Reincarnation as the method of spiritual evolution

At this point, it's obvious that the 2 theories of life presented above are equally unacceptable to any thoughtful person. Therefore, we are going to consider the idea of reincarnation as the most logical theory of life that explains all the differing circumstances seen in the world.

To best understand this, it will be important to re-cap what we covered in chapter 1. As we have already learned, we are all immortal spirits, pure consciousness, and fragments of the Divine. As fragments of the Divine, we hold all possibilities of development within us. And, as we have seen, *the plan for our spiritual evolution is to awaken our latent abilities into active powers through ongoing and varied experience.* This experience occurs over eons of time in which we incarnate as different forms of life on plane after plane of our solar system in order to learn to vibrate in response to all the possibilities of life.

So, when we look around us today, we now have a plausible explanation for all the varied circumstances of life that at first looked so confusing. If we accept that we are souls on a journey of spiritual evolution that spans hundreds of physical lifetimes, we can then understand that different people will naturally be at different points in their spiritual evolution (*just like there are students at every grade level in school*). And we can also understand the teaching of the Wisdom Tradition that tells us all the varied circumstances of life are perfectly suited to the evolution of each individual soul. For example,

- *There are baby souls who are still learning the basics.* They are making a lot of mistakes and generating a lot of bad karma. These are the souls that take birth in primitive or violent cultures. They are learning many lessons about survival. And those individuals that choose to be selfish and cruel to others are learning that pain and suffering always follow their harsh actions.
- *There are the younger souls who are making some progress in their evolution but are still attracted to material pursuits.* These types are born into

materialistic cultures in which they pursue their thirst for money, power and possessions. Although this is a higher level than the baby souls, these individuals still have much to learn. Eventually, they will find the *selfish* pursuit of materialism always leads to unhappiness and suffering.

- Finally, **there are the older souls who are working on more advanced topics**. These are the unselfish and kind-hearted people that don't care whether they have - or don't have - material possessions; because no matter what their wealth or position, they will use everything they have in service to the world. These are the true philanthropists, teachers and healers of the world.

Planning for a new life

Now that we understand a little more about the evolution of the soul and the absolute need for reincarnation in order to learn all the lessons that physical life has to teach, let's get back to where we left off earlier – the point at which our soul planned its next lessons and is ready to descend into another physical life.

At this point, reincarnation pushes the soul back down through the lower levels of existence, picking up all the bodies that it will need for its next life on earth. This will require adding a body on the Mental, Astral and Physical Planes, in that order. Once that is done, the soul finds itself taking birth in the family and surroundings best suited for its new lessons; and begins its journey through another life.

For most people, **this process of reincarnation will continue for many hundreds of lives until we learn all the lessons that earth life has to teach. After that, the soul will break the wheel of karma and will no longer need to incarnate in the physical** *world.* But this doesn't mean we are finished with our schooling only to move into some sort of spiritual retirement and decay. On the contrary, once this stage is reached, another and higher series of "lives" awaits us as our soul begins to evolve through super-human experiences on the higher planes of existence until even the soul itself will be transcended and only the immortal spirit or "Monad" remains to begin a life of infinite growth and evolution among its peers. The Monad never knows death, even when the manifested universe ends and a time of rest, assimilation and planning takes place before the next universe comes into being. That's because our spirit is of the very essence of the Divine and its immortality is assured.

Our infinite, immortal life

We have come now to the point at which we can begin to appreciate the teaching of the Wisdom Tradition that tells us we are all "Sparks of the Divine Flame". And, regardless of our level of development, we can gain peace through the realization that we are all immortal, and that our consciousness can never be extinguished. There is a future of infinite growth and infinite possibility awaiting us. A future of immortality in which *There is No Such Thing as Death.* And *that* is something we can all look forward to.

> *There is no devil; there is no hell; there is no angry god; and there is absolutely no death. There is only an eternal life of infinite creative possibilities given to us from a loving Universal Force, in whom, in very truth, we live and move and have our being.*

HOW TO VERIFY

THE WISDOM TRADITION

FOR YOURSELF

∞ **Chapter 7** ∞

Developing Clairvoyance

Verifying the Wisdom Tradition for yourself

Now we come to the fun part: learning how each of us can begin to develop clairvoyance. In this chapter we are going to look at the powers of observation we already possess and discover ways we can steadily improve them so we can begin to verify some of the teachings of the Wisdom Tradition firsthand. To make this process as comprehensible as possible, we are going to break it into 3 steps:

Step 1: Review our current powers of observing the world
Step 2: Look at a definition of clairvoyance
Step 3: Walk through the proven methods for awakening our higher senses

Step 1: Our powers of observation

There are two ways to improve our power to observe the world around us: *improving our instruments* or *improving the observer*. Let's take a look at what these different methods entail.

1) Improving our instruments

This method is what our scientists use. They develop finer and more precise instruments to examine the physical world (*things like better microscopes, computers and telescopes*).

2) Improving the observer

This method, which has been known about and practiced throughout history in the East, seeks to improve the observer by developing what are commonly called psychic or clairvoyant powers. And through these awakened powers, a developed person can observe much more of the physical world than any scientific instrument ever likely to be developed. The reason for this statement is because these awakened powers are super-physical and can therefore see rates of vibration beyond the observational capability of any physical instrument.

For example, with astral vision we can blow up an electron to fill our entire field of vision and examine it in minute detail as if we were standing right next to it! So, the day when science begins to partner with clairvoyants, our lives will be immeasurably improved because much knowledge that is now hidden will become available.

Step 2: A definition of clairvoyance

The stereotypical view of clairvoyance is that it has something to do with the degraded practices of psychic hotlines, mediums, and fortune tellers. And, as we have already learned, that is not what we are talking about in this book. Instead, we are going to take a look at *trained clairvoyance*, which is a completely different thing. First, we need to realize that clairvoyant abilities are the birthright of every human being; and that these powers can be developed in anyone through careful training. But one of the greatest barriers to its widespread development is social pressure that tells us, "clairvoyance doesn't really exist" or, "clairvoyance isn't normal".

All these thoughts are simply *limiting beliefs*. They are forms of negative programming designed to hold humanity back from awakening to the wider life all around us. How many times have you been told that you can't do something; but, once you really put your mind to it, you found that you actually *could* do a great job? It is exactly the same thing with clairvoyance. Don't let anyone tell you that you can't develop these abilities, because **you *can* develop clairvoyance if you are willing to work at it.**

So, what is the clairvoyance that we will be talking about in this book? Let's start with a definition: *Clairvoyance means "seeing clearly", but for our purposes it is more accurate to describe it as perceiving clearly.* It includes what we would normally associate with seeing, hearing, smelling, tasting, and feeling on a much higher level. In everyday language, ***clairvoyance is the ability to perceive a greater range of vibrations from the world around us than the average person.***

For example, we have all been taught that the human eye can only see what is described as the "visible spectrum" of light that runs from red to violet; and that the human ear can only hear what is called the audible range of sounds. Well, that simply is not true.

It *is* true that the vast majority of people can only see or hear within a certain range, but it is *also* possible to develop our senses – both physical and super-physical – so that we can perceive vibrations that used to be invisible to us; such as infra-red and ultra-violet rays, plus "sounds" and "colors" that exist on the planes of nature that lie outside of the Physical Plane.

Step 3: Yoga practice as a proven method of developing clairvoyance

People in the East have been using yoga to develop very high forms of clairvoyant abilities for thousands of years. For evidence, all we have to do is turn to the Yoga Sutras of Patanjali.(10) This book was written down around the year 400 AD but existed in oral tradition in India long before then. *The Yoga Sutras contain specific descriptions of the super-physical accomplishments (siddhis) that are developed by anyone who devotes their life to a raja yoga practice.* Some highlights include:

- *super-physical hearing, touching, seeing, tasting and smelling*
- *reviewing the past and seeing into the future*
- *remembrance of past lives*
- *reading other people's thoughts*
- *astral travel*

These are just a few of the abilities that come to the devoted yoga practitioner; and they are abilities that will come to anyone who takes the time to develop themself ahead of the curve by practicing *true* yoga. What true yoga really is, we'll discover in this chapter. But we can be sure it is much more than the physical postures that most people associate with yoga today.

At this point, the question you might have is, "How can I start to develop some of these abilities myself?" And the short answer is, *All of these clairvoyant abilities can be achieved by the awakening of faculties that lie dormant in every human being.*

Methods for awakening our higher senses through yoga

When most people think of yoga, they think of going to a local yoga class where a bunch of people wearing tight, trendy clothing are going to engage in a contest of flexibility while seeing who can sound the most spiritual by repeating certain fashionable phrases or sayings.

As a former yoga teacher, I can tell you that the classes that only focus on the physical postures are not true yoga by any stretch of the imagination. Unfortunately, in the West, many yoga studios have chosen to focus on the physical postures while sprinkling on a light dressing of spirituality to make it seem like it's more than just another method of bodybuilding; which is all that it really is. And while there is nothing wrong with getting into great shape in a yoga class, it's important to realize that yoga practice was meant to be much more than that.

Yoga means "union", and ***true yoga is - and always has been - a spiritual practice that seeks to unite the "lower self" with the "Higher Self".*** The yoga postures we are familiar with are just one tool used in the process of yoga; and the purpose of the postures is to help purify and strengthen the body to prepare it for a more effective and safe meditation practice. But there are also many other practices of purification besides yoga postures that will help us along our path to clairvoyant development that we will review in just a minute.

The Higher Self

But first, to help clarify the concept of "lower self" and "Higher Self", lets refer again to our chart of the 3 lowest planes of nature.

The 3 Planes of Current Evolution

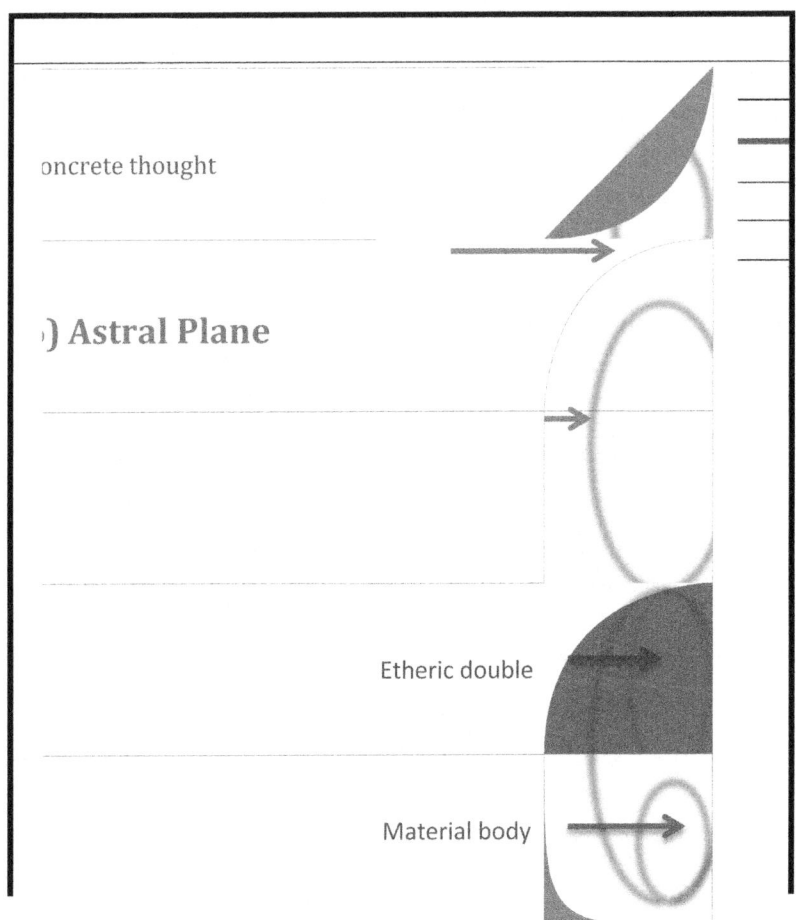

oncrete thought

) Astral Plane

Etheric double

Material body

The "lower self" consists of the 3 lower bodies that our soul "wears" (the physical body, the emotional body and the mental body); while the "Higher Self" is represented by the soul. (*The soul is also triple in its nature and has parts of itself that exist on planes 4 and 3 (the Intuitional and Spiritual Planes) but it is enough for us to realize that our "Higher Self" is the part of us that exists above and beyond the mental, emotional and physical bodies.*)

Purification and meditation

Getting back to our discussion regarding the best way to develop clairvoyance, we are going to find that the proven method of awakening our higher senses is straightforward. It involves a comprehensive yoga practice that anyone can master.

There are 2 main components to this process – *purification and meditation*. The purification process helps us to clean up the vehicles (bodies) that we currently have so they can perform better and become more sensitive to higher vibrations. Then, the meditation process helps us reach upward toward the Higher Self. Meditation teaches us to still the body, emotions and mind so that inspiration can flow down from higher planes directly into our lives.

The combination of purification and meditation is very powerful, and everyone who follows the process is sure to get some result. So let's take a look at what it involves, starting with purification.

Purification

The purification process requires "cleaning up" the 3 bodies we use to perceive the world around us: the physical, the astral, and the mental bodies. In other words, we need to purify our thoughts, desires, and actions. And by purifying ourselves we increase our sensitivity; first to the physical world around us, and later to the super-physical worlds that surround and interpenetrate the Physical Plane.

Purifying our thoughts means thinking only good and helpful thoughts towards others and towards ourselves. It also means getting rid of the mass of self-centered thoughts that surround most of us and replacing them with thoughts of service.

Purifying our desires or emotions means curbing our lower, self-focused desires and replacing them with higher, other-focused desires. Examples of low desires include lust, greed, obsession with material success, and social status; while examples of higher desires include unconditional love, compassion, and devotion to a high ideal. We should also be careful about our choices in entertainment realizing that most of the programming on television, in the movies and on the Internet is designed to manipulate us emotionally through violence, hyper-sexuality, intrigue, greed, materialism, etc.

Purifying our actions means purifying our physical lives. This includes avoiding gluttony, addiction, and cruelty. In addition, we need to be careful of anything we put *into* or *onto* our bodies, like what we eat, drink, and breath; cosmetics; our physical environment; close friends; places we frequent; and our sex behavior.

For easy reference, the following table summarizes the guidance on purification.

Self-purification on the 3 Planes

- **Physical purification**
  - o **Eat, drink and breathe healthy** – the yoga books say, "no alcohol, tobacco, or meat". For our purposes, let's do the best we can to move toward an organic, plant-based diet, reduce or eliminate alcohol, and don't smoke or vape anything.
  - o **Daily exercise** – the body should be in excellent physical health. Establish a regular daily routine with at least 30 minutes of moderate to vigorous cardiovascular exercise. Better still, take walks or runs in a park and disconnect from digital pollution (*e.g. no cell phones or headphones*). Enjoy nature and slow down a little.

- **No toxic chemicals on the body** – this includes most cosmetics, anti-perspirants and sunscreens. Instead, choose natural cosmetics, natural deodorants (*anti-perspirants block the pores and contribute to cancer since toxins back up into lymph nodes located under the arms*), and natural sunscreens (*mineral-based or clothing, hats, umbrellas, sunglasses*). Better yet, enjoy the sun in the morning or evening hours <u>without</u> sunscreen when the UV index is 3 or lower and stay in the shade during mid-day. It's actually healthy and very important for us to get some sun exposure since the sun carries several important life forces (like prana) as yet unknown to science that help heal and sustain the body and uplift our spirits.
- **No drugs** – neither recreational nor pharmaceutical unless they are absolutely essential for health (*like taking insulin or heart medication*). Most pharmaceuticals can be reduced or eliminated with a healthy diet and exercise or replaced with natural alternatives. Work with your doctor, a dietician or herbalist for help with this. If your doctor won't help you reduce medication intake, find one who will. Osteopathic doctors, known as DOs, can be a good start. DOs are trained in both traditional medicine and natural methods that allow the body to heal itself.
- **Choose friends and associates wisely** – toxic people – whether friends, work associates or even spouses – can pull us down no matter how hard we work for the good. It is essential to our success to surround ourselves with supportive and loving

people, even if it means leaving a job or ending a relationship. And *anyone who shows a pattern of abusive behavior – physically, emotionally or mentally – needs to be removed from our lives immediately.* If you need help with this, ask for it. There are many support groups available.

o **Sex behavior** – It's ok to enjoy sex; just be sure it's with someone you care about and the purpose is mutual upliftment, joy and shared intimacy. (*Here's any easy way to adopt this practice: plan to never have sex with someone unless you are completely sober. If we need drugs or alcohol to have sex with others, that indicates underlying psychological issues that should be addressed with a healthcare professional*)

o **Do no harm to human beings, animals or the planet** – cause no *physical* suffering to people, animals, or the planet. This is more than just avoiding physical violence and includes things like eating a compassionate diet and making informed choices about the products we buy and the companies we support.

- **Emotional Purification**
  o **Eliminate fear-based emotions** such as: depression, anger, lust, jealousy, envy, malice, and pride. To do this, focus on the opposite quality that you are looking to develop. For example, if struggling with depression, make a gratitude list every day and do something to help others (*when we are helping those less fortunate, we can't be depressed. This is a proven method for reducing*

feelings of depression). If we have trouble with anger; focus on practicing patience and sending loving thoughts to others. To overcome pride, focus on ways to practice humility.

- o **Cultivate love-based emotions:** even if we think we are already doing well in this area, keep working on practicing kindness, compassion, empathy, love, encouragement, humility and devotion to a high ideal

- o **Entertainment - Don't watch TV** except for a few uplifting or educational programs. Selectively choose news sources, movies and Internet-based entertainment – Most of the mass media are sources of fear-based programming and are designed to incite the lower passions (*e.g. sex, envy, malice, violence*) *and* keep us in a state of passivity

- o **Do no harm to human beings or animals –** cause no *emotional* harm to others or animals. This includes stopping non-constructive criticism, manipulation, harping, threatening, or controlling behavior when dealing with people; and providing a sense of security and love for animals.

- • **Mental Purification**
  - o **Eliminate constant self-centered thoughts** about what we want to get out of life, obsession with material success and social status, and what others should be doing according to our opinions and plans. Replace these thoughts with serenity, acceptance, and empowered choices that allow us to take care of ourselves and help others.

- o **Think of what we can *give* at every point of the day.** This gets us out of ourselves and is proven to improve our mood and outlook on life
- o **Focus on thoughts of gratitude** for whatever life brings our way. Although it may not feel that way at the time, everything is working together to help us on our spiritual journey
- o **Do no harm to the world** – cause no *mental* harm to people, animals or the planet by ceasing any negative thoughts towards those around us. As we have learned, thoughts are real things, so we need to remind ourselves to send out thoughts of love, support, strength and encouragement (*Yes, even to animals and to plants*).

Although these instructions may sound like a lot to tackle, don't worry about trying to achieve perfection all at once. Just do the best you can to work at these items piece by piece. And while you are practicing these principles, remember that the best strategy for adopting a new habit is repetition. The more we do something, the more it becomes second nature.

If you find that following these suggestions is difficult, don't worry, that's normal. We grow up in a culture that encourages self-centeredness, individual achievement, and competition. So, it takes time to change old habits. But, if you are ready for a better life, and excited to start experiencing the higher realms of reality for yourself, here are a few insights that will help you along the way.

First, it's important to realize that clairvoyant training is not a form of severe self-discipline. If anything, it is the height of common sense and follows what is called the middle path. For example, the choice is not between the rampant, self-indulgent sex life promoted by the mass media or a life of complete celibacy locked away in a remote religious retreat. Instead, it means that we respect others and ourselves enough to enjoy a true sexual bond with someone we care about. (*And no, we don't have to be married, we just need to approach sex from a perspective of mutual respect.*)

How purification awakens clairvoyance

A logical question at this point might be, "Why would purifying ourselves in thought, desire and action awaken clairvoyant abilities?" This is a good question – and I had the same thought myself – so here's the explanation:

When we indulge continuously in self-centered thoughts and desires, we create what can best be described as "clouds" of thought and desire matter that form a barrier to letting in higher vibrational thoughts and emotions. These "clouds" are actually *thought forms* that we produce by the power of our own thought. The stronger and more persistent thoughts create lasting forms that a clairvoyant can see hovering around every individual. It is as if we built an invisible cage around ourselves. And these cages "color" and bias our views of the world and other people, just like a pair of colored sunglasses tint everything we see. But, once we begin to think more of others and less of ourselves, we literally begin to break down the cage that separates us from the higher vibrational realms, and we become increasingly open to receiving (*reading*) other people's thoughts and emotions.

Likewise with the physical body. When we poison it with alcohol, drugs, tobacco, and meat obtained through cruelty, we coarsen our senses and become dull to the vibrations of the world around us. And just to be clear, this statement is not meant to be moralizing in any way; it simply states the results that follow from consuming those things. For example, alcohol and tobacco actually produce a hardening of the etheric double, which dulls the ability of the physical body to receive vibrations from the higher worlds. Meat that comes from animals that are mistreated on factory farms causes 2 unpleasant side effects: First, we get the karma associated mistreatment; which means a portion of the suffering and premature death of the animal is transmitted to us (*as we saw in chapter 1*). And second, we actually absorb some of the life force of the animal that is carried in its blood; and this lower life force tends to pull us down into lower vibrational behavior patterns, making us more prone to aggression.

From a more motivational standpoint, consider this: that **alcohol, drugs, tobacco and meat have been promoted to us for many generations** for 2 reasons:

> 1) so a few individuals and large corporations can make a lot of money, and
>
> 2) to *intentionally* keep our senses dull in order to control us. The goal being to keep us focused on the physical plane and our lower desires to turn us into consumers who purchase material goods in order to satisfy the desires created by advertising and other promotional strategies.

You may initially be skeptical about this whole process; but why not give it a try and see what happens? Again, these recommendations are about practice, not perfection. Just do the best you can to move in a positive direction. You can always go back to living as before. But don't quit until you've started to experience at least the early stages of clairvoyance because the whole world will start to look very different; and what you see will amaze you! *The world is much more than it appears to be, and there is a tremendous amount of life that is hidden from us, even on the purely Physical Plane.*

Attracting a teacher

More important than improving our ability to read peoples emotions or thoughts is the possibility of something even more amazing. If we dedicate ourselves to following the path of purification and service, <u>we will start to get help on our journey.</u> Throughout history, this has been known as "walking the path" or "finding a guru". This is no fiction that we might hear about in a yoga class, but an absolute reality that is open to anyone who is willing to step away from a life of materialism and devote themself to personal development in order to be of greater service to the world.

Suffice it to say, through steady hard work along unselfish lines, each one of us will attract the attention of a teacher who will be more than happy to guide us toward the development of wider abilities for service to the world, including development of clairvoyant faculties. And we most definitely do not need to fly to India or hike through the Himalayas in search of a guru. That idea is nonsense promoted by those whose consciousness is focused on the Physical Plane. <u>No one can buy their way to spiritual advancement</u> just because they can afford a flight half way around the world. No such physical search is necessary.

Anyone who is committed to living the life of purification and service outlined above will attract the attention of a teacher. And it's absolutely impossible that anyone could be overlooked because someone who devotes themself to selfless service stands out like a bright beacon of light on the higher planes of nature in comparison with average humanity. In fact, we could live in the most remote part of the planet, and if we practiced unselfish service to others and longed for teaching in order to make ourselves of greater service, the teaching would come.

The old saying is absolutely true, "When the student is ready, the teacher will come". As much as this may sound incredible to many people, I can vouch for its truth since it happened to me. After dedicating myself to the path of yoga for a year and a half, a teacher came forward that helped focus my efforts in certain directions that allowed me to become of greater service to the world and awaken the beginnings of clairvoyant abilities.

Meditation

Now that we have a good idea about the importance of purifying ourselves physically, emotionally and mentally, the next step requires the development of a regular meditation practice. Meditation can often be confusing to many people who are not accustomed to it. And even though we hear a lot these days about the importance of meditation, very few people know what it really is and what kind of results to expect. However, in this book we are going to make it easy and break it down into 2 types of meditation that anyone can practice: a simple method and a more advanced method.

First of all, effective meditation is an essential part of a true yoga practice. And that means that the goal of our meditation is creating the union of the "lower self " and the "Higher Self". In essence it is a spiritual process that helps us realize the existence of the Higher Self and allows us to begin to guide our lives by higher inspiration rather than by the lower desires.

This is a big challenge for most people because we have been taught that "who we are" resides in our minds. Well, that simply is not true, and we can prove it to ourselves through meditation. In meditation we learn not only how to still the physical body, but also how to quiet our thoughts and emotions so inspiration can begin to flow down from the Soul into our waking consciousness. Once this happens – and just the smallest amount of inspiration flows down from the higher planes – the result can be life-changing, because *we begin to realize in very truth that the mind is just a tool in the hands of our Soul or Higher Self, and that there really is an immortal part of ourselves that lives on after the death of the physical body.*

So, now that we know what effective meditation is all about (*union of the higher and lower selves*), let's take a look at two types of meditation you can use to develop your clairvoyance.

Technique #1 - Simple breath meditation

This method is perfect for beginners and it's easy to do. Find a regular place to meditate free from disturbance and noise. Start with some gentle stretching exercises to help get any tension out of the body (*e.g. reach for your toes; stretch side to side; take your hand and gently stretch the head and neck forward, then back, then side to side; sit in a chair and do some spinal twisting to the left and then to the right*). Assume a comfortable seated position whether in a chair, on a bed or on the floor with your back straight (*laying down tends to put us to sleep, so it is always better to sit*). It is also important that the spine be in a straight, upright position (*not slouched or bent*). Use a cushion or backrest to support your back. Feet should be flat on the floor if you're in a chair or in a comfortable cross-legged position if you're on the floor or in bed. You don't have to be in full lotus position, just comfortable crossed legs. (*If you have any trouble keeping the legs crossed and find your circulation feels cut off, go ahead and straighten both legs out in front of you*). Hands should rest one on top of the other in your lap with the palms turned upward. Wear earplugs if there are any noise distractions. Close your eyes. Relax your jaw. Teeth should be slightly apart and not clenched. Release the tongue from the roof of the mouth. Gently inhale and exhale taking long, deep breaths and using a sounded breathing technique (*slight constriction at the back of the throat so the breathing sound is audible*). This will create a subtle "white noise" effect. Breathing should be gentle and steady (*not forced or rapid which can cause light-headedness*). Focus just on the sound of the breath or the cool feeling of the breath in the back of the throat. That's all there is to it. If thoughts come in, acknowledge them and let them float by and return your attention to the breath.

The goal is to become the "witness" or "observer" of our thoughts, emotions and body. We watch the breath and we watch our thoughts, but we do not identify with them. Start with just 5 to 10 minutes of this type of meditation. Then, work up gradually to 20 - 30 minutes depending on how much time you are able to devote to your practice. Over time this meditation technique helps us to realize we are more than our "lower selves". We start to recognize there is a part of us that exists above and beyond even our thoughts. This is the beginning of identifying with our "Higher Self". And although this breath meditation is simple, it is actually very powerful and effective.

If persisted with, this meditation technique can lead to very meaningful results. Over time, you may begin to feel that you lose track of time; that you go "somewhere else" and return to your physical body. Later still, you may begin to get glimpses of life on the Astral Plane.

Technique #2 - Advanced meditation

The advanced meditation technique involves 2 steps:

Step 1 - Concentration

Begin by practicing concentration. Concentration is just focusing the mind on one thing without letting the thoughts wander. Start with some gentle stretching exercises to help get any tension out of the body (*e.g. reach for your toes; stretch side to side; take your hand and gently stretch the head and neck forward, then back, then side to side; sit in a chair and do some spinal twisting to the left and then to the right*). Then, sit in a quiet meditation position and as described above. Pick an inspirational object of concentration. This can be a person, a thing, or a virtue. Some people can just close their eyes and imagine a tree, or a waterfall, or a person of high spirituality that they look up to. Others, who have trouble visualizing, should use a picture to focus on. Then, close the eyes and keep the image in mind. Start breathing as described in the simple meditation technique. It is normal for our thoughts to wander. Just gently bring them back to the object of concentration as many times as needed. Also make sure that the physical body does not become tense during concentration. *(This is natural since we often associate concentration with wrinkling the brow or stiffening the body. But that kind of physical tension must be completely avoided. Concentration takes practice and you should not get discouraged.)* As the mind wanders or the body stiffens, just bring the mind back and relax the body. Keep the breath gently moving.

Start with just 5 minutes a day. If that becomes easy, gradually move up to 10, then 15 minutes. Once you get to the point at which you can truly concentrate on one thing for a full 10 minutes without your mind wandering, then you are ready for meditation. *(Note: you should never stare at candles or images for long periods with the eyes open as some methods of meditation recommend. These methods may indeed cause a certain trance state, but they will damage your eyes and put you into a passive state approaching mediumship, which is dangerous to your well-being since they run the risk of obsession by an astral entity. Therefore, these practices are not recommended)*

Step 2 - Meditation

Once concentration is mastered, it is time to start meditation. Begin just as in concentration by focusing on an inspirational object or person of your choice without the mind wandering. But this time, try to reach up into the object of meditation. Try to merge yourself into your vision of the highest aspiration you can imagine. Think of becoming one with that higher Consciousness in whatever form it takes (*for some this may be a religious figure; for others it may just be the sheer majesty of the universe; just pick an inspirational subject that works for you*).

At first your attempts will likely be unsuccessful, but don't give up. Each time you practice you will get a little closer to succeeding. Then, there will come a day when you feel that you leave your body and merge into that higher Existence, if only for a moment.

From this point forward life will never be the same. Each time you meditate you will find yourself able to spend more and more time in the higher planes. And with this development, you should increasingly be able to bring back memories of what you have seen.

[*As a word of caution, these glimpses of the higher worlds may lead to a brief time of unconsciousness. There is nothing to be afraid of and this is perfectly natural. That's why it is important to meditate in a chair or in a seated position that will keep you upright or allow you to tip sideways without injury.*]

Practice makes perfect

One final thought on meditation. In order for it to be effective, the best method is to practice every day at the same time. The ideal time is early morning since this is usually the quietest time of day; plus, we are still somewhat connected to the higher planes when we first awaken. But if this time doesn't work, an alternative would be right before going to bed at night. Just pick what works best for you and make sure you practice regularly. I found it helpful to schedule my meditation as a recurring appointment on my calendar so I see it every day and get a reminder to set aside that time for practice.

Some important tips

Now that you have a basic idea about how to develop clairvoyance through purification and meditation, here are a few tips to help speed the process.

1) Recognize a Higher Power – in whatever form works for you

Above all, it is important that we recognize that we do not succeed in life by ourselves. This is the beginning of the end of our self-centeredness; which, as we know, is essential for clairvoyant development. For some, this Higher Power may be God; for others, the Spirit of the Universe; and for still others some form of Group Consciousness. No one is here to tell you what that is. The key is to remove self-centered thoughts and replace them with gratitude for all the help that is given to us every day. Knowing this, we can practice living in a state of gratitude to the Universal Force that sustains us all because we understand that everything in life is designed to work for our spiritual evolution, even the challenges and sadness that may come to everyone at some point in their lives.

2) Live a life of service

Similar to what was said earlier, this does not mean we have to run away from the life we know and join a religious order. It simply means recognizing the unity behind all life and **taking**

every moment in our daily lives as an opportunity to be of service to the world; this could mean physical things like helping others or caring for animals and the earth. And it also includes sending positive thoughts out to the world on a regular basis, as well as supporting people emotionally through all the joys and sorrows of life.

Summarizing the process of clairvoyant development

The methods outlined above may not be exactly what you expected. Maybe you imagined there was some sort of secret teaching for rapidly developing clairvoyance. Actually, there are a number of psychic development schemes out there that promise to quickly awaken some forms of clairvoyance through the use of drugs, dangerous breathing practices, and kundalini yoga. People who develop along this path run a very real risk of injuring themselves physically, emotionally and mentally; and any clairvoyance gained in this manner is always lost in the next physical life. Plus, we have to consider the bad karma that is generated by following the path of selfishness.

But if you practice the methods for clairvoyant development described in this book, you can rest assured they are perfectly safe. The slower and safe way to develop psychic abilities is the method that has been shared with students of the white path throughout history; and I can vouch for its effectiveness and safety since this is the method that was taught to me (and which I have used for 11+ years without any trouble). Importantly, any abilities you gain in this lifetime by following the white path will adhere to the soul and become its permanent possession in future lives. Therefore, you are investing not only in developing current abilities, but also in carrying forward abilities that will make you more effective in fulfilling the opportunities for service that come your way in future incarnations.

If you asked me to boil down the whole method of developing clairvoyance into a simple phrase, it would be:

Purify your physical, emotional and mental natures; meditate on the Higher Self; and practice selfless service to the world.

What to expect

In the early stages of clairvoyance, all you may experience is a slight, but noticeable change in your perception of the world. *Colors will start to look a little brighter. Sounds will get a little clearer. Your senses of smell and taste will improve, and your sense of touch will become finer.* Enjoy these experiences and keep working at your growth; things will keep getting better!

Later on, *you may start to notice that you are better able to tune into the feelings of others.* You may be able to sense their inner emotions and be able to tell if they are happy or sad even if they try to hide it. See what emotions you can notice in other people and in animals. Observe them, don't judge, meditate on your experiences, and keep practicing.

Later still, *dreams often become clearer.* You may increasingly find they start to have a regular sequence to them. This is a very good sign, since it indicates you are able to bring more and more of the experiences you are having on the Astral Plane during sleep into your waking memory. (*Keeping a dream journal can help with this process and is amazing to look back on as you start accumulating more and more of your nightly adventures*) You may even find that a few of these "dreams" turn out to be prophetic, and come true in the near future. If you get to this stage, you're really close; keep working at it.

Eventually, the early signs of a higher clairvoyance may start to dawn. ***Solid objects may start to look slightly transparent.*** You may see what look like little atoms dancing around on the surface of *and within* what is supposed to be a "solid" table. If you are at this stage, very soon you may start to see the "auras" around people. Keep in mind that the "aura" is not one thing but is composed of multiple bodies: the etheric double, the astral body, and the mental body. For example, most people usually start to see the etheric double first since this is still a manifestation of our physical body, though invisible to most. (*It looks like a light bluish-grey or purplish-grey mist that extends about ¼" from the physical body all around, and it is best seen by slightly unfocusing the eyes and looking just beyond an exposed area of skin in dim lighting.*)

Next, you may start to see the astral body. This is built of a much finer type of matter, but it is so much brighter and more colorful than the etheric double that many people see it at about the same time as the etheric double or even sooner. (*The astral body appears as rapidly rotating bands of color that extend about 18" from the surface of the body in roughly the shape of an egg*). **If you get to this stage, then you will be able to clearly read the emotions of other people** (*because each emotion has a unique color associated with it which you will learn to interpret over time*).

Later still, and with continued practice, you will begin to see the mental body. This much finer part of the aura also extends about 18" from the body and appears as an egg shape just like the astral body; except the colors of the mental body are more stable and form themselves into steady bands and regions of color that reflect the persistent patterns of thought for an individual.

At this point, if you have developed the sight of the mental body, you will be able to read the thoughts of others; and it will no longer be possible for anyone to deceive you when it comes to their real thoughts and intentions.

How long will it take?

The length of time until you can expect to see results varies depending on the level of development of your soul and the amount of effort put into the method of awakening clairvoyance outlined above.

For example, there may be souls who have made considerable efforts in developing clairvoyance in previous lives. As a result, in this life they may make rapid progress. If you are one of these people – and you can already sense emotions in others or maybe even see some of the human aura – it may be a matter of months to a few years to unfold astral clairvoyance.

For others who have not developed these abilities in past lives and are approaching this material for the first time, it may take many years of very hard work just to get to the beginning stages of clairvoyance. But never get discouraged! ***Everyone who persistently works at the process of clairvoyant development along the lines of selfless service outlined above is sure to get <u>some</u> result in this life.*** Not all of us may get visions of life on the Astral Plane, but we can certainly make considerable progress toward improving our sensitivity to the world around us; including gaining an ever-widening appreciation for the feelings of others. (*Just imagine all the things in life that you could enjoy even more if you had improved sight, smell, taste, touch, and hearing!*). The important point to note is that, even if we all don't gain the ability to see life on the astral plane, we can at least have initial experiences that prove the truth of some of the basic teachings put forward in this book (like beginning to see the faint bluish-white glow of the etheric double just beyond the tips of the fingers). Once you gain even this small step, it lends believability to the other teachings about the higher planes that may be out of reach, but that will come to all of us in the course of time if we persist with our practice of healthy living coupled with meditation.

A personal story

My experience is very modest. I was always somewhat sensitive to the world around me since an early age; but I never possessed anything that could be considered clairvoyance. In fact, I spent most of my early adult years in the pursuit of the material life, and didn't start practicing yoga and working at clairvoyant development until I was in my 40's. But once I started, I worked persistently (*every day*) at clairvoyant development using the methods described in this book and here's what I found during the first 6 years of practice:

- Colors got brighter. All my other senses started improving. My head felt clearer and I felt more connected to the earth.

- I became more sensitive to the feelings of others and animals. I had a teacher come into my life that made suggestions on how to continue to grow along spiritual lines.

- The sky started to look more alive. On certain days when there were only thin, wispy clouds, it felt as if there were living forces at work behind some of the shapes and patterns. There was also a feeling that somehow these experiences in the sky were also taking place inside of me. This is very hard to put into words, but it was as if I felt a temporary expansion of consciousness that also included things that were far away. These feelings did not occur every day; but they did happen most days when I went to the beach or for a hike and found a quiet place to rest and meditate on the sky. At this point I also started to lose interest in what people would normally think of as material success; like having a certain job, salary, house, car, spouse, etc.

- People began to change. Of course, *they* really didn't change at all, it was just my perception of them that changed. It became more and more clear there are many things that other people are able to hide from us. But now I began to see through some of the exterior projections and see more of who they really were on the inside. Surprisingly, some of the people who used to appear so beautiful and seemed to have everything, were many times the ones who started to look the most "empty" and "false"; while others who appeared very simple on the surface started to look "brighter" and more "real".

- My dreams started to become more organized. I often recognized entire sequences of events that were happening in a different world. I had many dreams of flying and floating in which I could move rapidly across a landscape or downstairs without my feet ever touching the ground. A few of these dreams turned out to be prophetic and foretold of future events. (*These events were nothing special, just regular encounters with people I knew that came true a few days or weeks after the dreams took place*). Little by little, I also started to get glimpses of the etheric double. If I stared at my hand in dim light I could see a bluish-white light extending just a little beyond my skin all the way around. I could also see very brilliant particles of light zipping and dancing around a clear blue sky on a sunny day if I held my eyes slightly out of focus.

- I also started to develop tinnitus (a ringing in the ears) that my teacher explained was the beginnings of clairaudience. When I meditated, more and more I would begin to hear faint sounds. Most of these were just many layers of beautiful harmonies at a very high pitch (almost out of the range of hearing). At this point, life began to feel transformed. Events started to become more synchronous. People and things would come into my life exactly when I needed them. And events that initially felt like failures and setbacks turned out to be amazing gifts that opened up new doors. I started to feel I was being taken care of, and that all I needed to do was concentrate on ways of being helpful to others and the rest would take care of itself.

A few notes on tinnitus

More than ever, there are people in the world that are experiencing tinnitus, or ringing in the ears. There are even Internet radio stations that claim their programming will help relieve tinnitus; along with ads online promising various "cures". While some of forms of tinnitus may result from physical causes – such as disease or injury – a large number are the result of a mass spiritual awakening that is taking place on the planet. I share this information because there is a lot of confusion and fear around these symptoms and we are often taught to look for drugs or surgery as a solution.

I am not here to diagnose any individual case – that is something between you and your doctor – but if you are otherwise very healthy, it may be worth considering the fact that tinnitus can indicate the beginnings of clairaudience. This is something a doctor would not understand, but you would sense it inside as true.

In my case, the initial ringing in my ears was faint. But I was prepared for it, and not afraid. In fact, I would intentionally meditate on the sound and try to go further into it to see if I could hear more. Over the course of about a year the single high-pitched sound I heard became more and more complex; until it eventually opened out into a fuller, more harmonic sound. I now hear a high-pitched sound constantly, day and night. My understanding is that this will continue until I eventually gain the ability to hear life on the Astral Plane. In the meantime, I am not the least concerned about it.

The yoga culture – choose carefully

In the world today there is a deep longing for spiritual connection. This can be seen in the rise of the yoga culture and the founding of small, self-sustaining communities. This is a beautiful sign! But unfortunately, as with any major social trend, there are individuals and corporations that look upon these events as money-making opportunities.

As a former yoga teacher, I have observed that much of the yoga offered today places an over-emphasis on physical postures with a superficial nod to spirituality. You can tell the teachers and studios that fit this description by their focus on the purely physical aspects of yoga. Some of these studios even promote events and retreats that include alcohol, partying, and self-indulgent materialistic behavior. So, if you decide to take yoga classes, be sure to look for a teacher or studio that supports you on your soul's journey. Use your intuition and good judgment; it's worth making the extra effort to connect with a group of like-minded people.

And just like there is corruption in the yoga community, there are many individuals who promote psychic or clairvoyant development along the faster, but more dangerous paths mentioned earlier in the book. Some of these may be well-meaning people who simply have no idea about the dangers associated with premature psychic development. However, there are others who follow the left-hand path – or dark path – and seek to develop clairvoyant powers for their own selfish use in order to gain advantage over others. This type of development is very real and not just a fiction that belongs in the movies. ***No words of caution can be strong enough to impress upon everyone the need to stay away from any classes or teachers that follow the left hand path***.

The dangers of kundalini yoga

For example, there are yoga studios and teachers today that offer "kundalini yoga". This may sound harmless enough to someone unfamiliar with kundalini but read on and you may change your mind. Kundalini is a very real etheric force that resides at the base of the spine. When aroused, it usually flows up the spinal column and awakens some of the chakras, which in turn open up certain types of clairvoyance. But this type of awakening should only be done under the guidance of a qualified teacher (*who will never charge for this kind of spiritual advice*).

The force of kundalini is not to be taken lightly. It is a resistless force that can burn through physical tissues and cause tremendous pain. But this physical damage is the least of its dangers. The greatest risk is not that it will burn its way up the spine and shoot out the top of the head (which usually happens); but that it will move downward and outward through the chakra associated with the sex force, magnifying those cravings to the point that they turn its victim into a monster of lust (*yes, really*). And this effect is not just a passing thing that happens for a weekend but may persist for weeks, months or even years.

Therefore, any teachers offering group kundalini classes are to be avoided. Either they have no idea what the force is they are dealing with (*which is probably true in most cases*); or they have some knowledge of kundalini and are following the dark path, taking as many students down with them as they can.

But don't worry about the dark side people. As was already mentioned, we function in a universe that operates under Divine Law, and we are each responsible for our thoughts, emotions and actions. If someone selfishly uses clairvoyant abilities for personal gain they face two harsh realities: first, *all the negative karma generated has to be paid back through suffering*; and *second, they run the risk of falling further and further down the dark path*, each fall making it harder to get back on track. Therefore, your best strategy is to avoid these people and practice sending out good thoughts, which repels those who are functioning on the lower levels of consciousness.

Final words of inspiration

I hope this journey through life, death and the structure of our universe has been eye opening and enlightening! Although many of the topics described in the book may be new, give them time to sink in. In fact, you could try the method suggested to me when I first started reading books on the Wisdom Tradition, which stated, "*Each book should be read a minimum of seven times. Reading more times than that would further deepen and widen understanding.*"

This may sound overwhelming at first. But I found that as I re-read the material at my own pace, I eventually did read some of the books 7 times; while others I am still working on. It's an ongoing process and any student of the higher life should not be worried about how much time it might take since we know – as immortal spirits – we have all the time we need; and that our progress along the path of spiritual development unfolds based on our own effort (or lack thereof). Our future is literally in our own hands since we are each the makers of our own destiny.

We can be 100% certain that in this world – as in the entire universe – there is perfect justice. No one ever gets more or less than they deserve. We each create our future circumstances by the thoughts, emotions and actions we allow ourselves to indulge in today. This is the Law of Karma in action and it reflects a very simple underlying truth. As difficult as it may be to realize at times, we are all interconnected and part of the same amazing Substance that interpenetrates and sustains the entire universe. And *literally EVERYTHING is part of that same Substance; the earth, the air, the plants, the animals, the sun, the planets, etc.*

Once we learn this lesson of unity in its fullness, we will be free from the necessity of rebirth on earth. But until that time, the more we practice developing Unity consciousness, the more our lives will take off; and the sooner we can create a life of joy beyond our wildest dreams.

This doesn't mean we have to be perfect at this stage in our evolution. We are not saints. But *the goal is to recognize more and more that what we do to others and the world around us we actually do to ourselves.* This is a difficult concept to grasp in our self-driven culture. We feel so separate and alone sometimes; even when surrounded by people. But we can begin to move in the direction of recognizing our interconnection with the world through the little things we do every day. How we treat other people – not just physically, but emotionally and mentally. So besides just holding the door for someone, let's send them helpful thoughts and emotional support.

The more we practice these principles, the more we begin to see the results in our day-to-day lives. *It changes us.* We start to feel a new sense of peace and happiness. And, if we observe carefully, we will see that uplifting thoughts sent to someone else actually show up on their face or in their body by a slight "brightening". We can see them straighten up or maybe even give a slight smile. And the more we practice, the more the evidence will mount until we begin to see that *thoughts are real things* and that **what we think about makes a difference in our lives and the lives of others every day.**

If fact, realizing that thoughts are real things will usually be the first proof most people receive that some of the concepts described in this book are correct. And even if just one or two things come true, then it increases the likelihood the other statements are also correct.

The doors to a new life

So why not start living a life of *giving back* that is more in harmony with the world around you? We can each work at purifying our lives and meditating on a regular basis. There's nothing to lose and so much to gain. As you practice selfless service to others your efforts will begin to awaken your higher powers of perception. ***You will start to develop clairvoyance and begin to verify for yourself that There Is No Such Thing as Death, because you will feel it in your heart, and you will see it with your awakened higher senses.***

In love and service,
A. Zimmerman, PhD

References

1) C.W. Leadbeater. (1929). *The Monad and other essays upon the Higher Consciousness.* Adyar, India: Theosophical Publishing House. Online edition: www.anandgholap.net.
(p. 21) "In the course of various investigations it has come in our way to examine some thousands of human beings."

2) C.W. Leadbeater. (1912). *A textbook of Theosophy.* Adyar, India: Theosophical Publishing House. Online edition: www.anandgholap.net.
(p. 7) "Theosophy has its aspect as a science also; it is in very truth a science of life, a science of the soul. It applies to everything the scientific method of oft-repeated, painstaking observation, and then tabulates the results and makes deductions from them. In this way it has investigated the various planes of nature, the conditions of man's consciousness during life and after what is commonly called death. It cannot be too often repeated that its statements on all these matters are not vague guesses or tenets of faith, but are based upon direct and oft-repeated *observation* of what happens."

3) C.W. Leadbeater. (1895). *Astral plane. It's scenery, inhabitants and phenomena.* Adyar, India: Theosophical Publishing House. Online edition: www.anandgholap.net.
(p. x-xi). "I worked at it for forty-two days, and seemed to myself to be on the brink of the final victory, when the Master Himself intervened and performed the final act of breaking through which completed the process, and enabled me thereafter to use astral sight while still retaining full consciousness in the physical body – which is equivalent to saying that the astral consciousness and memory became continuous whether the physical body was awake or asleep. I was given to understand that my own effort would have enabled me to break through in twenty-four hours longer, but that the Master interfered because He wished to employ me at once in a certain piece of work.

"Psychic Training
It must not for a moment be supposed, however, that the attainment of this particular power was the end of the training. On

the contrary, it proved to be only the beginning of a year of the hardest work that I have ever known. It will be understood that I lived there in the octagonal room by the river-side alone for many long hours every day, and practically secure from any interruption except at meal-times. Several Masters were so gracious as to visit me during that period and to offer me various hints; but it was the Master Djwal Kul who gave most of the necessary instruction. I know not how to thank Him for the enormous amount of care and trouble which He took in my psychic education; patiently and over and over again He would make a vivid thought-form, and say to me: "What do you see?" And when I described it to the best of my ability, would come again and again the comment: "No, no, you are not seeing true; you are not seeing all; dig deeper into yourself, use your mental vision as well as your astral; press just a little further, a little higher.

"This process often had to be many times repeated before my mentor was satisfied. The pupil has to be tested in all sorts of ways and under all conceivable conditions; indeed, towards the end of the tuition sportive nature-spirits are especially called in and ordered in every way possible to endeavour to confuse or mislead the seer. Unquestionably it is hard work, and the strain which it imposes is, I suppose, about as great as a human being can safely endure; but the result achieved is assuredly far more than worth while, for it leads directly up to the union of the lower and the higher self and produces an utter certainty of knowledge based upon experience which no future happenings can ever shake."

4) C.W. Leadbeater. (1895). *Astral plane. Its scenery, inhabitants and phenomena.* Adyar, India: Theosophical Publishing House. Online edition: www.anandgholap.net.
(p. 2). "...every precaution in our power has been taken to ensure accuracy, no fact, old or new, being admitted to this manual unless it has been confirmed by the testimony of at least two independent trained investigators among ourselves, and has also been passed as correct by older students whose knowledge on these points is necessarily much greater than ours. It is hoped, therefore, that this account of the Astral Plane, though it cannot be considered as quite complete, may yet be found reliable as far as it goes.

"[Thus I wrote some forty years ago in the first edition of this book; now I may add that daily experience during the whole of that time has but confirmed the accuracy of last century's investigations. Much that was then still somewhat strange and novel has now become familiar through constant and intimate acquaintance, and a mass of additional evidence has been accumulated; here and there may be a few words to add; there is practically nothing to alter.]"

5) C.W. Leadbeater. (1912). *A textbook of Theosophy.* Adyar, India: Theosophical Publishing House. Online edition: www.anandgholap.net.
 (p. 16). "After some years of work I had the privilege of coming into contact with these great Masters of the Wisdom; from Them I learnt many things – among others, how to verify for myself at first hand most of the teachings which They had given. So that, in this matter, I write of what I know, and what I have seen for myself. Certain points are mentioned in the teaching, for the verification of which powers are required far beyond anything which I have gained so far. Of them, I can only say that they are consistent with what I do know, and in many cases are necessary as hypotheses to account for what I have seen. They came to me along with the rest of the theosophical system upon the authority of these mighty Teachers. Since then I have learned to examine for myself by far the greater part of what I was told, and I have found the information given to me to be correct in every particular; therefore I am justified in assuming the probability that that other part, which as yet I cannot verify, will also prove to be correct when I arrive at its level."

6) **What is dark energy?** (n.d.). *NASA*. Retrieved June 12, 2023 from: https://science.nasa.gov/astrophysics/focus-areas/what-is-dark-energy
(para. 3). "It turns out that roughly 68% of the universe is dark energy. Dark matter makes up about 27%. The rest - everything on Earth, everything ever observed with all of our instruments, all normal matter - adds up to less than 5% of the universe."

7) C.W. Leadbeater. (1929). *The Monad and other essays upon the Higher Consciousness.* Adyar, India: Theosophical Publishing House. Online edition: www.anandgholap.net.
 (p. 42). "One of the greatest causes of suffering in our present life

is what we are in the habit of calling our separation from those whom we love, when they leave their physical bodies behind them. Having only his physical consciousness, the un-instructed man supposes himself to have "lost" his departed friend; but this is really an illusion, for the departed friend stands beside him all the time, and watches the variations of feeling expressed in his astral body. It will at once be seen that it is impossible for the departed friend to be under any delusion that he has "lost" the loved ones who still retain physical vehicles, for since they must also possess astral bodies (or those physical vehicles could not live) the "dead" man has the living fully in sight all the time, though the consciousness of his living friend is available for the interchange of thought and sentiment only during the sleep of that friend's physical body. But at least the "dead" man has no sense of loneliness or separation, but has simply exchanged the day for the night as his time of companionship with those whom he loves who still belong to the lower world."

8) C.W. Leadbeater. (1929). *The Monad and other essays upon the Higher Consciousness.* Adyar, India: Theosophical Publishing House. Online edition: www.anandgholap.net.
 (p. 38). "The journey still takes an appreciable time, even though the amount is small and we can reach the other side of the world in a few minutes."

9) About. (n.d.). *Dr. Jim B. Tucker.* Retrieved June 12, 2023 from: www.jimbtucker.com
"Jim B. Tucker, M.D. is Bonner-Lowry Professor of Psychiatry and Neurobehavioral Sciences at the University of Virginia. He is Director of the UVA Division of Perceptual Studies, where he is continuing the work of Dr. Ian Stevenson with children who report memories of previous lives. A board-certified child psychiatrist, Dr. Tucker worked with Dr. Stevenson for several years before taking over the research upon Dr. Stevenson's retirement in 2002."

10)   Satchidananda. (1978). *The Yoga Sutras of Patanjali, Translation and Commentary by Sri Swami Satchidananda.* Reprint, Yogaville, VA: Integral Yoga Publications, 2011.

Suggested Reading List

The structure of our solar system, the planes of existence, and the method of spiritual evolution

Outline of Theosophy, by CW Leadbeater
(excellent for the beginner)
Textbook of Theosophy, by CW Leadbeater
(for intermediate students)
The Rosicrucian Cosmo-Conception, by Max Heindel
(for advanced students)

The Astral Plane (the intermediate world) and the Thought Plane (the Heaven world)

Astral Plane, by CW Leadbeater
The Devachanic Plane, by CW Leadbeater
Life After Death, by CW Leadbeater

Reincarnation and our life between lives

Reincarnation, by Dr. Annie Besant
Life Before Life, by Jim B. Tucker, MD
Return to Life, by Jim B. Tucker, MD
Journey of Souls, by Michael Newton, PhD
Destiny of Souls, by Michael Newton, PhD
Life Between Lives, by Michael Newton, PhD

Karma

Karma, by Dr. Annie Besant
A Study in Karma, by Dr. Annie Besant

Clairvoyance

Clairvoyance, by CW Leadbeater

The super-physical abilities that result from raja yoga practice

The Yoga Sutras of Patanjali, by Sri Swami Satchidananda

Glossary of Terms

For a better understanding of the following terms, please refer to the chart of the 7 Planes of Consciousness in Chapter 1.

Astral body – one of the 3 "bodies" that our soul wears to experience life. It is made entirely of astral matter, which belongs to the 6th plane of nature, the Astral Plane. Through the astral body we are able to experience all the emotions of life. We also live in the astral body for a time after death equal to about 1/3rd of our earth life.

Astral Plane – the 6th plane of our solar system (counting from the top down) that lies closest to the Physical Plane that we know. The Astral Plane can be divided into 3 major groupings. The lowest astral (containing the 7th sub-plane or underworld); the middle astral (sub-planes 6, 5, and 4); and the upper astral (sub-planes 3, 2, and 1), known as the "Summer Land" or 1st Heaven.

Etheric double – the invisible counterpart to our material body. Every particle of the etheric double is an exact duplicate of our material body. In fact, it is sometimes referred to as the etheric mold because the etheric double comes into existence *before* the material body (which is built up according to the pattern established in the mold).

Mental body – one of the 3 "bodies" that our soul wears to experience life. It is the source of the human mind and home of all that we know of as "thought". It is made up of matter of the 4 lowest sub-planes of the Thought Plane. We also live in the mental body on the lower thought sub-planes (or 2nd Heaven) for a period of time that varies widely based on the unselfish forces put in motion during earth life; varying from barely a touch for a brutal, selfish person up to 1,200+ years for someone of high spirituality.

Physical Plane – the lowest plane of Nature in our solar system (plane #7). This is the plane we are all familiar with. It contains both the physical matter that we are aware of (solids, liquids and gasses from the lowest 3 sub-planes) and etheric matter (which constitutes the highest 4 sub-planes that interpenetrate all physical matter).

Planes of Nature – there are 7 planes of Nature in our solar system, each containing matter of a certain density vibrating within a certain frequency range. For example, the Physical Plane is the 7th and lowest plane, and the one we are most familiar with. There are also 6 planes above the physical. As we go up the planes, we find decreasing densities of matter and increasing rates of vibration. We also find that we have the ability to perceive increasing dimensions of space as we go up the planes. Trained clairvoyant investigation has confirmed there are 7 dimensions of space in our solar system. On the Physical Plane, we are only able to appreciate 3 of them. On the Astral Plane we are able to perceive 4 dimensions; the Thought Plane 5; the Intuitional Plane 6; and the Spiritual Plane 7. Beyond the spiritual plane, space and time as we understand them have no meaning.

Soul – the relatively permanent part of us, whose lowest expression exists on the upper 3 thought sub-planes. Our soul contains the memory of all our past lives on earth and knows all the qualities that it needs to develop in the future.

Sub-plane – There are 7 planes of Nature in our solar system. Each one of these planes can be divided in turn into 7 sub-planes that represent matter of varying degrees of density and vibration *within* the plane.

Thought Plane – the 5th plane of our solar system (counting from the top down). It is a realm of pure thought that is divided into 2 large segments: the 4 lower sub-planes being the home of our mental body and the realm of concrete thought; while the 3 upper sub-planes are the home of the lowest manifestation of our immortal Soul and home of abstract thought.

About the Author

A. Zimmerman, PhD is a university professor, active yoga practitioner, and devoted student of the Ancient Wisdom. His writing style reflects the methods used in the classroom: an informal, conversational approach coupled with the use visual highlights, charts and examples that make the subject matter come alive. He has practiced the methods of clairvoyant development outlined in the book and has achieved results that exceeded his expectations. His goal in life is to share what he has learned with others so they can begin to awaken their own inner abilities.

It is simply a matter of how hard we work which determines the rate of development of clairvoyant abilities; and because of that fact, the principles taught in this book about the after-death states are truths which you can begin to verify for yourself.

There Is No Such Thing As Death
provides a beautiful and transformational perspective on life,
death and the mysteries of the universe.

**There is no such thing as "dead matter"; and
there is absolutely no such thing as a single star in
the sky that does not have life associated with it
in one form or another. In fact,
THERE IS NOTHING BUT LIFE, EVERYWHERE.**

*The idea that we are alone in the universe is absolute
nonsense promoted by those who would keep humanity living
in isolation and fear. The reason for this should be obvious.
When people are afraid, they are easier to control, and they'll
go along with whatever those in power tell them to do.*

*But the moment we realize who we really are - and take
back our heritage as creator beings on a magnificent journey of
discovery - is the minute we break free from our prison of
limited thinking. Once this change in perspective sinks in,
life begins to take off in unimaginably beautiful ways.
No longer are we helpless victims looking for someone else to
save us. Instead, we realize that the earth is exactly what we
have collectively made it. And the sooner we take responsibility
for this creation and start working to improve it,
the sooner we will see a new golden age dawn on earth.*

Printed in Great Britain
by Amazon

60788308R00088